BEGINNIN

Every day more and more pe
mystical realms of life. While son
warded, too often the seekers find themselves lost, ... g
frustrated, and overwhelmed. Because of this, Dragonhawk
Publishing has established BEGINNINGS, a series of books to
guide the true seeker safely into the realms of wonder, mystery, and human possibility.

Whether seeking psychic power, effective healing tools
and techniques, a closer connection with Nature, or a greater
realization of your own inner potentials and creativity, there
are two important keys. The *first key* is realizing that this is
not just for the few and gifted. Everyone has the ability to
develop that potential.

The *second key* is having the right teacher. To this end,
DragonHawk Publishing has enlisted internationally recognized author, storyteller, and mystic Ted Andrews to shepherd
this series. One of the most dynamic teachers and leaders in
the field today, he touches thousands upon thousands every
year through his books and his seminars.

All journeys begin with the first step. Whether truly a
beginner or one who has walked the path, our BEGINNINGS
series will help you experience and renew the wonders of yourself and of life. You will safely explore new realms and new
possibilities. And you will realize a truth that all seekers eventually uncover:

We are never given a hope, wish, or dream
without also being given opportunities
to make them a reality!

Alan Michaels
CEO
Dragonhawk Publishing

BEGINNINGS:
A DRAGONHAWK SERIES

Music Therapy
for Non-Musicians

Elaine,
May your heart
sing with joy!

by
Ted Andrews

Ted Andrews
9-14-97

DRAGONHAWK PUBLISHING   BATAVIA, OHIO

A Dragonhawk Publishing Book

Musical Therapy for Non-Musicians.
Copyright ©1997 by Ted Andrews

First Edition

Cover design by Ted Andrews

Editing and book design by
Pagan Alexander-Harding (IAAI, Hitterdal, MN) and
Diane Haugen (Whiskey Creek Document Design, Barnesville, MN)

ISBN 1-888767-31

Library of Congress Catalog Card Number: 96-071460

This book was designed and produced by

Dragonhawk Publishing
P.O. Box 275
Batavia, OH   45103-0275
USA

ABOUT THE AUTHOR

Ted Andrews

Ted Andrews is an internationally recognized author, storyteller, teacher, and mystic. A leader in the human potential and metaphysical fields, his books have been translated into nine foreign languages, and he is often featured on both national and local television and radio programs.

A teacher and counsellor in the public school system for ten years, Ted has an extensive formal and informal education. He has been involved in the study of esoteric, the occult, and holistic health for over 30 years and is known for his dynamic and practical seminars and his ability to make the mystical accessible to everyone.

Called a true Renaissance man, Ted is schooled in music, and has composed, performed, and produced the music for over a half dozen audio cassettes. He has worked as a holistic healer, with a focus upon creating individualized musical therapies, and Ted is also a continuing student of the ballet and Kung Fu. He holds state and federal permits to work with his own birds of prey, and conducts animal education and storytelling programs throughout the United States.

TO WRITE TO THE AUTHOR

Ted appreciates hearing from readers, learning of their enjoyment and benefits of his books. Letters to the author may be sent to the following address:

Ted Andrews
c/o Dragonhawk Publishing
P.O. Box 275
Batavia, OH   45103-0275

Other Titles by Ted Andrews

Dragonhawk Publishing Titles

Treasures of the Unicorn
More Simplified Magic (spring 1997)
Psychic Protection (summer 1997)

Music and Spoken Audio

Roses of Light
Upon the Wings of Angels
Mystery of the Fire Spirits
Uncover Your Past Lives
Psychic Protection
Discover Your Spirit Animal
Entering the Tree of Life
Sacred Rites of the Seasons
Enchantment of the Faerie Realm (forthcoming)
Developing Psychic Touch (forthcoming)

Books by Ted Andrews through Llewellyn Publications

Simplified Magic
Sacred Power in Your Name
How to See and Read the Aura
Dream Alchemy
How to Uncover Your Past Lives
Sacred Sounds
How to Meet and Work with Spirit Guides
How to Heal with Color
Magickal Dance
Enchantment of the Faerie Realm
The Occult Christ: Angelic Mysteries & the Divine Feminine
Animal-Speak
The Healer's Manual
How to Develop and Use Psychometry
Crystal Balls & Crystal Bowls

TABLE OF CONTENTS

Ted Andrews   vii

ILLUSTRATIONS

TABLES

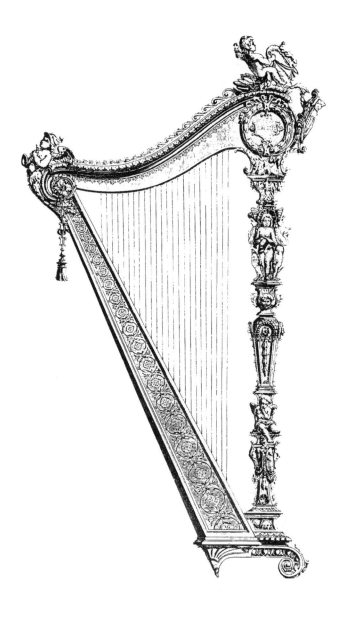

MUSIC THERAPY FOR NON-MUSICIANS

Introduction

There was once a man who was successful in all things. He had a fine wife, a loving family and a craft for which he was justly famous. But still he was not happy.

"I want to know Truth," he said to his wife.

"Then you should seek her," she replied.

So the man put his house and all of his worldly goods in his wife's name, (she being adamant on this point). Then, he went out on the road, a beggar and seeker of Lady Truth.

He searched up the hills and looked down in the valleys for her. He went into small villages and large towns; into the forests and along coasts of great seas. He went into grim dark wastelands and into lush meadows strewn with flowers. He searched for days, for weeks, for months and for years.

And then one day, at his point of greatest frustration, he stood atop a high mountain. As he looked down upon the earth below him, he doubted that he would ever find his Lady Truth. And it was at this point that he noticed a small cave to his left. As he looked into the mouth of the cave, he saw an old woman sitting upon the dirt floor.

She was a wizened old woman with but a single tooth left in her head. Her hair hung down onto her shoulders in long, greasy strands. The skin on her face was as brown and dry as old parchment. Her prominent bones seemed to protrude through that old skin.

She looked up as he stood in the mouth of the cave and signaled to him with a hand cragged and arthritic with age. But when she spoke in greeting, her voice was so soft and lyrical that it touched his heart. And in that moment he knew he had found Lady Truth.

He stayed a year and a day with her, and he learned all that she had to teach. And when the year and day was up, he stood once more at the mouth of the cave ready to leave. He looked at her upon that dirt floor and he was filled with emotion.

"My Lady Truth," he said, "you have taught me so much. You have healed my life. Is there not something that I can do for you?"

Lady Truth put her head to one side and brushed a greasy strand of hair from her old eyes and considered his request for a moment. Then she looked at him and smiled her near toothless smile.

Yes," she said. "When you speak of Lady Truth to others—as you will—tell them I am young and beautiful!"[1]

---

[1] Adapted from *Favorite Folktales from Around the World* by Jane Yolen. Copyright 1986 by Random House, Inc. Adapted by permission of Pantheon Books, a Division of Random House, Inc.

This is a wonderful time to be living. Much of what used to be considered the stuff of fiction, and much of what was once considered metaphysical mumbo-jumbo is now recognized to have strong threads of truth running through it. Today we also have the technology to verify what used to be scoffed at by the scientific community.

Since the beginning of time, every society has expressed its truths in a manner unique to that society. Regardless of how these truths were expressed, with just a little examination, common threads run through them all. When we hear or read about this phenomenon of common threads—especially in societies that had no contact with each other—it should make little bells go off in our heads. Learning about these common threads should give us great pause for thought. They tell us something very universal is going on here, something very wonderful— something we need to be paying attention to!

One of those common threads found in all traditions and societies are the teachings of the sacred power of sound, music, and voice. The use of sound to create healing changes in oneself or in others is found universally.

Chinese healers used singing stones—thin flat pieces of jade which would emit various musical tones when struck or played like a xylophone. The Sufis consider *hu* to be the ultimate creative sound, chanting and singing it to create changes in consciousness. The Tibetans considered *kung* to be the great tone of Nature. Sculptures in Baghdad (circa 4000 BC) show musicians with harps and flutes. Egypt had entire choruses and orchestras by the time of the pyramids. Shamans in many aboriginal and native societies use drums and rattles to heal the body and to touch other realms. Chanting, singing, praying, rattles, drums, and flutes—every aspect of sound was recognized for its ability to effect changes in body, mind, and spirit.

In our modern times, the ancient mysticism of sound and music may be lost to conscious thought to the average individual. But the truth and reality of the healing power of music is still experienced by everyone. How often have we heard a song from the past, only to be transported for a few brief moments to the time period that we associate with that song? How often do we hear a song and suddenly we feel sad or even very romantic? And what about the music that makes us tap our toes or want to get up and dance? This is but a small reflection of the magic and power of sound.

Some music can move us to tears, while other music makes us want to dance. Some music agitates and irritates us, while other music arouses us. Some

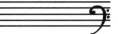

music and sounds make us tense, while other music and sounds soothe and relax us.

We can't help but respond to music. We are each musical beings. The gift of music lives within each of us. We have been surrounded and nourished by music since the moment of conception—from the sounds carried to us through the amniotic fluids during pregnancy to the strong rhythmic beat of our hearts. Music and rhythm are inherent to our very being.

Sound is a contributing factor to our present state of health and consciousness. The difference between the random sounds of daily life and the focused use of healing sounds is that the latter will produce or restore harmony. Every part of our being has the capability of responding to sound and music. Every organ and every system within us have their own rhythm and musical resonance. If an organ or system is off key or out of balance, we can use sound, music, and voice to help restore harmony to the organ or system that is affected.

Music is healing, and each of us can use it to strengthen the body, mind, and spirit. It doesn't require great musical knowledge or extensive musical training. Simply by understanding a few basic principles and applying some basic techniques, we can each apply music and sound to our health mainte-

nance. We can each learn to employ rhythms, tones, instruments, vocalizations—separately or in combination—to interact with the physiological systems of the body. We can literally tune ourselves up—starting today!

Tuning ourselves with sound, music, and voice will affect each of us differently, but it will affect us. To heal with music though, we must participate in it as we did as children. This involves more than just listening to it or using it to fill voids within our lives. We must examine it and work with it from an entirely different perspective. We must remember that within music are the keys to the wonders and miracles of life. Within music are all of the principles of life—physical and spiritual.

People are frequently amazed at how simple, and yet how effective, sound healing can be. Maybe it's because we live in a technological society, and thus we have come to expect everything to be complicated. What is so wonderful about sound and music therapies (as with most vibrational therapies) is that we do not have to fully understand how they work to experience their effectiveness. Very few people understand how electricity works, but that does not prevent any of us from using it to our benefit. The same is true with sound healing and music therapies.

It is for this reason that I chose not to give any more theory than is necessary in this handbook. Instead I tried to focus on what is practical and usable by the average individual. The exercises included will enable you to experience the various effects of sound and music in healing the body, mind, and spirit. If you need more explanation or greater understanding of theory, refer to the bibliography. Many of the works listed provide a wonderful source of additional information.

Exercises and therapies included in this workbook are NOT meant to be prescriptive. Nor are they meant to be a panacea for every illness and problem that arises. They are guidelines only. When followed, we experience the reality of vibrational healing through sound and music.

Take the guidelines and exercises and test them. Reshape them and adapt them to yourself. Don't be afraid to resynthesize them into a sound method that works for you as an individual.

People who experience healing through unorthodox manners often exclaim, "The most amazing thing happened!" The truth is that our prayers are supposed to be answered. Miracles are supposed to happen and healing is supposed to occur. The truly amazing thing would be if they did not!

It is not the knowledge, not the power or might,
but the simplicity of application
that is the wisdom of the sages...[1]

Edgar Cayce

---

[1] Edgar Cayce. *A Garland of Wisdom*, comp. W.H. Church (Virginia Beach, Virginia: A.R.E. Press, 1975), p. 17.

Chapter 1

Holistic Health and Sound Healing

Healing is fastest and most effective when we incorporate all aspects of our being. We are more than just physical creatures. We have emotional, mental, and spiritual dimensions as well, and each of these has an impact upon our overall balance and well-being. These other dimensions make us such wondrous beings to begin with. Recognizing and working with these other dimensions involves a personal commitment on our part. It means we must take responsibility for our overall health,

On the surface, we seem to live in a very health-conscious society. However, when we look below the surface, we will find many people do not know how the body operates or how we can most effectively help it to maintain a healthy balance. The human body is truly magnificent; it knows how to take care of itself. Unfortunately, we often get in its way through our habits and our ignorance. How often have we, or our friends, tried to get ourselves in shape and had the following scenario occur?

We decide to initiate a good health maintenance program for ourselves. We begin to exercise and eat properly. We get lots of fresh air. Then, four to six weeks into the program, we come down with a cold or the flu. We become confused as to how this could happen. After all, we've been doing the right thing. We have been good about taking care of ourselves lately, so how could we be getting sick?

The answer is rather simple. For a long time prior to initiating our health program, we neglected ourselves in the variety of ways humans typically do. As a result, toxins built up in the body. These toxins could be from the foods we ate or from the negative emotions and mental attitudes we mistakenly assumed This in turn weakened the body's overall resistance. When we began our healthy regimen, these toxins were stirred up.

The toxins in our bodies are similar to the silt that accumulates at the bottom of a river, building up over time. During rains or other times when the river begins to flow more strongly, the silt is stirred up and brought to the surface. A healthy regimen often stirs the body's toxins that have settled within us, bringing them to the surface so they can be cleaned out. We "come down with a cold" or "catch the flu." The runny nose and fever indicate the body is being stimulated to cleanse itself of accumulated silt or toxins.

In reality, the runny nose and fever are positive signs, actually confirming that our better health regimen is working. If we continue our regimen and allow the cleansing to run its course, our body's cleansing process will usually be completed in three to seven days. Unfortunately, many assume these are negative signs and become discouraged, using this as an excuse to discontinue the regimen. As a result, our ignorance of the processes the body uses to maintain health and balance can create problems for us.

Quick Fixes

We live in a *fast-food* society. We like to pull into the drive-through window, pick up what we need with no fuss or bother upon ourselves or our time. People will catch a cold with irritating symptoms, such as a runny nose, and the first thing they do is buy an over-the-counter medication with an antihistamine to stop the runny nose. Although the medication will help ease or eliminate the symptom, it does not cure the problem.

A runny nose is the body's natural way of cleansing itself. When we interfere with the body's cleansing process rather than assisting it, we push the problem deeper into the body where it will only resurface more strongly at some other time. On the other hand, if we allow it to run its course, supporting and strengthening the body with such things as proper fluids and nutrition, the cleansing process will

complete itself. As a result, we can become stronger and healthier than we may have been in a very long time.

Effective holistic health practices begin with a greater awareness of how the body operates and maintains itself. Over the years, I have taught a great number of holistic health workshops and seminars, including the proper use of herbal, sound, color, and aroma therapies. I am always surprised how unaware the average person is of the human body—its organs, systems, and their basic functions. I am frequently amazed when someone does not know the difference between a gall bladder and a urinary bladder, assuming they are just different names for the same organ.

We need to keep in mind that most of us will be living in our bodies for eighty or more years. The more we know about how our body operates, the easier it will be to take care of it and to live a healthy life. This does not mean that we have to know all of the technical, biochemical-biomedical aspects required of physicians and other health practitioners. But every one of us should be, at the very least, familiar with the body's organs, their functions, and location, along with the emotions and mental attitudes most strongly affecting their operation. It might also be useful to become more aware of our body's natural weaknesses, strengths, and genetic predispositions.

Taking Responsibility for Our Health

In the past, many people have given over the responsibility for the care of their own bodies to the physician. While it is true that most physicians know more about the technical data of the human body than the average individual will ever know, no one knows more about your body than you do. This is not to say that we don't need physicians. We do. However, no one knows more about what affects you emotionally, mentally, spiritually, and physically better than you.

Unfortunately, we are not taught to acknowledge or pay attention to the intimate communications we receive daily from our bodies. Many people seem unwilling to take the time to learn about themselves. To them, it seems easier to give that responsibility over to someone else. They would prefer to hire the physician to fix them when they get sick or to know what is needed for their health rather than know for themselves.

This fast-food approach to our health has its repercussions. In many ways, it can lead to our thinking along the lines of "if only we could hire someone to eat for us, go to the bathroom for us, or even breathe for us—after all, we are so very busy." This sounds good in theory, but in practice it is ineffectual. The effects and repercussions for our health regimen and

maintenance fall upon our own shoulders. No matter how many people we hire to care for bodies, we should always be the primary care-giver!

All Healing Comes From Within

All healing comes from within. Our genetics, certain social influences, and other factors may predispose us to certain kinds of illnesses and imbalances. Orthodox medicine can serve as a magnificent catalyst for alleviating a problem, but orthodox medicine will not always correct the cause of a problem.

Asthma and allergies, for example, run in my family. As a child, the asthmatic episodes were often quite intense and difficult. Today, even though I still occasionally have asthmatic episodes, the triggers are more definable. Knowing this predisposition, I work regularly to strengthen my possible weaknesses and to prevent as much trouble with them as possible.

Since I know my lungs are my weak point, I do extra work with them to keep them strong. I exercise my lungs regularly (with both aerobic and anaerobic exercises). I also am aware of tendencies toward certain emotional disturbances that are more likely to trigger asthmatic episodes. Because of this, I take extra care in handling those emotions more effectively and in avoiding those types of situations as much as possible.

Be Aware of Your Health Weaknesses

By examining your family medical history—in conjunction with your own individual medical history—you can usually determine your unique predispositions to various physiological patterns and psychological issues. By interviewing your parents or grandparents, you may determine the emotional and mental issues that run in your family. In turn, this knowledge can give you an awareness into your predisposition(s) to other health problems that can result from day-to-day stresses.

Again, to use myself as an example, in my family there is a tendency for all of us to have problems with issues of strength of will. Some had no will, some too much, some fluctuated. In my own case, I tended to exhibit an imbalanced expression of will. If someone told me to do something (whether it was the right thing to do or not), I would usually do the opposite simply because I was not about to be told to do anything. On the other hand, if the person asked me to do something, that was a different thing entirely. Had I not recognized and corrected this tendency earlier in my life, I would probably be still getting myself in a great deal of trouble.

To promote better health and well being, we must learn to take much of the responsibility for our own healing. There are times when orthodox medicine, including surgery, is very necessary to restoring health and balance, but to place the entire responsibility for our health in the hands of someone who does not live within our body is rather foolish. To make orthodox medicine the exclusive modality of caring for our health implies that healing can only come through certain individuals. This way of thinking sends a message to our own subconscious that we have no power over our own health.

Keep in mind that even modern medicine is still unsure of how various diseases manifest. Why do they affect some people and not others? What makes some people more prone to illnesses and imbalances? Words such as *bacteria, virus,* or *weakened constitution* are not really explanations. Viruses and bacteria surround us all of the time, so why do we get sick at some times and not others?

If we intend to participate more consciously in our own healing process, we must begin to recognize the causes and aggravations of various imbalances that we experience. Learning how emotions and mental attitudes intimately affect the functions of the human body is critical to holistic healing.

Improving Health with Music and Sound

Sound and music are two of the easiest and most beneficial techniques for alleviating these day-to-day stresses on the body and can be used on a daily basis to address these problems.

As I state in the Introduction, we can find evidence of sound and music for healing purposes in many cultures, for many centuries. However, it is only in the last 50 years that the idea of using sound and music for therapeutic purposes has gained some popularity within the medical and mental health communities in the United States.

You may not be familiar with many of the recent advances in music therapy because currently we don't have a central location for efficiently gathering the information about sound and music for healing purposes. However, we can find recent articles in several well-respected news publications citing the use of sound and music for therapeutic or stress reduction purposes:

In March 1995, *Tennis* magazine carries an article about how champion tennis players (Gabriela Sabatini, Lori McNeil, and others) use music to enhance their mental preparation and soothe them before a match.[2]

In August 1995, the *Mayo Clinic Health Letter* highlights research where music was used to treat people with Alzheimer's and Parkinson's diseases. In some cases, they have found that

[2] Jim Loehr and Susan Festa Fiske, "Listen to the Music," *Tennis* (March 1995), p. 34.

people with Parkinson's disease who listen to music while walking seem to move smoothly. The article also states: "Music has helped people with Alzheimer's disease communicate and recall memories, perhaps because musical abilities seem to remain even when speech is lost.[3]

In January 1996, *The Journal of the American Medical Association* (*JAMA*) describes the positive effects of a music-facilitated program for 30 homebound, older adults experiencing systems of depression, distress, and anxiety.[4]

In August 1996, a *Wall Street Journal* article reports how some companies (Motorola, Inc.; Apple Computer, Inc., etc.) have used music during management training sessions to hammer home the value of teamwork. In workshops, Arthur Hull, a management consultant, trained in music, works with participants to create a song. Participants use instruments (drums and xylophones) to build on a simple rhythm and learn to play their part. During the session, they symbolically develop an understanding of the value of teamwork by actively participating in the creation of a song.[5]

These magazine articles are just a few of the many successes that have been gained by many people using music therapy or sound and music healing

---

[3] "Activity Therapy: Hobbies Do More than Just Pass Time," *Mayo Clinic Health Letter*, vol, (August 1995), p. 6.

[4] J. Gerontol, "Effects of a Music Therapy Strategy on Depressed Older Adults," *JAMA*, *273*, 17, p. 1318.

[5] Michael J. McCarthy, "A Management Rage: Beating the Drums for the Company," *The Wall Street Journal*, (August 13, 1996), p. A1.

techniques. Appendix A provides answers to some frequently asked questions about music therapy.

However, the focus of this book is not to convince you of the merits of music therapy. The purpose is to provide methods for employing sound and music therapies to alleviate stress, improve health, and to promote healing. These methods and techniques are based on my years of experience in practicing sound and music therapy with hundreds of individual clients.

The methods described in this book are not prescriptive, nor are they meant to replace or substitute for orthodox medicine. Music cannot be prescribed like drugs. These methods are simply therapies that can be used with great effectiveness, and often in conjunction with orthodox medical treatments.

Remember, all treatments have some validity. Part of our responsibility in maintaining our own health is to find the method or combination of methods that works best for us.

As you use this manual of self-help, you will come to realize the full benefits of music therapy. By practicing the techniques offered, we can learn that we can control and heal more aspects of our life than we ever may have imagined—physically and otherwise. Although no musical training or background is necessary to use the techniques described in this book, it might be beneficial to understand the basic principles. upon which music therapy is built and operates.

NOTES

Six Principles of Holistic Health

Holistic health involves examining the emotions and mental attitudes that affect us on physical levels. At the end of the day, for example, it is helpful to look back over the day's events and identify the various emotions and mental attitudes that we have expressed inappropriately or been exposed to. By doing this, we can then determine which organs and systems are more likely to have become stressed. We can then initiate simple holistic techniques to alleviate that stress. In this way, the stress is prevented from accumulating and eventually aggravating or manifesting a condition in the body.

Before any holistic modality can be employed, it is most important to truly understand the basic principles of holistic health. On the following pages you will find the six principles necessary to the holistic healing process. The better we understand them, the more effective we will be in our own health maintenance and in applying the techniques within this book. They are the foundation for ALL healing.

1. The human essence is ENERGY!

Energy cannot be destroyed. Energy can be diverted, transformed, and transmuted. It can take a variety of new expressions. It can be impacted upon by other expressions of energy, but no matter how it is impacted upon, energy cannot die.

2. Our essence is continually changing in response to the conditions of our life.

Our energy and health reflect our response to these conditions. Because of this, we must find the method or combination of methods that works best for us as individuals. We must find a way to restore or maintain balance on a daily basis in order to maintain our health and our vitality.

3. Healing must always involve the whole essence—physical, emotional, mental, and spiritual.

Health occurs naturally in response to balance within all parts of our being—body, mind, and spirit in conjunction with the environment and all that we encounter within it. All factors play a role in our overall vitality.

4. **Physical symptoms reflect imbalances in other parts of our being and in areas of our life that are impacting upon us.**

We may have a predisposition, but outside stresses can aggravate or even help manifest physical conditions of imbalance. Recognizing this helps us to eliminate and control those stresses more effectively.

5. **Healing is aided through understanding our basic health patterns, our strengths and weaknesses, and how stress affects them.**

Imbalances usually occur at times of stress and in areas of the body most susceptible to stress. An examination of our own health patterns will help us to recognize these. In this way, we can incorporate measures to regularly strengthen and protect ourselves against possible imbalances.

6. **Healing occurs quicker and more fully when we are responsible and participate in the healing process.**

Common sense plays an important part. Proper diet, regular exercise, fresh air, adequate rest, and relaxation are essential to our overall health and balance. In addition, we can employ a variety of holistic modalities that are available to us.

The Principles of Sound and Music Therapy

There are many principles of sound and music therapy. For the purposes of this guide, I have simplified or combined them into four principles to make their applications more easily understood. These four are the most essential to beginning your own music therapy work.

ONE:

THE PRINCIPLE OF RESONANCE

In music therapy, resonance is the ability for a sound vibration or frequency to reach out and trigger a response in the human body. Every cell within the body is a sound resonator. The cells that combine to make up the individual organs and the system the organs belong to have their own individual sound frequencies—frequencies they more easily respond to.

When there is illness or disease, the affected organ or system falls out of its natural vibrational range. When this occurs, sound vibrations can be applied to impact upon the unbalanced organ or system, bringing it back to its normal parameters. This forced resonance can help restore harmony to the affected area(s).

MUSIC THERAPY FOR NON-MUSICIANS

TWO:

THE PRINCIPLE OF RHYTHM

Rhythm is the pattern of pulses in music—rhythm is essential to music. Without it, there can be no music at all:

> Without rhythm to move a melody along, we would never get past the first note. No motion, no rhythm. No rhythm, no music.[6]

Rhythm reflects the pulse of life. Different rhythms affect the physiological systems and organs of the body in various ways. The rhythms of different instruments and types of music can be used to bring about improvements in the rhythms of our own organs and body systems.

---

[6] Winton Marsales, *Marsales on Music* (New York: W.W. Norton & Company, 1995), p. 22.

THREE:

THE PRINCIPLE OF PITCH AND TIMBRE

Pitch is the highness and lowness of a sound. The faster the sound vibrates, the higher the pitch. The slower the vibration, the lower the pitch. Different pitches are more likely to influence different systems and organs of the body. For example, the heart responds to a natural fourth.[7] In the key of C, this would be the tone or pitch of F (or the F key on a piano's keyboard).

Timbre is the distinct characteristic of a sound that enables us to distinguish one voice from another, one instrument from another. Different organs and systems are also likely to respond to the sound of different instruments.

---

[7] *Natural* indicates a note that is neither a sharp nor a flat, such as the white keys of the piano.

MUSIC THERAPY FOR NON-MUSICIANS

FOUR:

THE PRINCIPLE OF SOUND AS ENERGY

Sound is an expression of energy, and the human body is an energy system. Because of this, sound has the capability of influencing the body's natural energy patterns.

As a vibration, sound also has the capability of interacting with other sources of energy frequencies. These frequencies can be color, fragrance, electro-magnetics, and other energy expressions. Vibrations can help or hinder, block or amplify each other. For each system of the body, I will provide guidelines for combining sound and music with other compatible vibrational tools.

Chapter 1

All Energy Follows Thought

Once we experience music therapy, our lives can never be the same. An old occult axiom states "all energy follows thought." Where our thoughts go, so will our energies. When we work with any holistic health technique, we realize the truth of this axiom. Every thought, word and deed that we express or experience will take on greater significance. We recognize the subtle communications from our body every time we express or experience an emotion or mental attitude. We become aware that life and energy are flowing and shifting within us and around us on many levels.

When we change our imaginings, we change our world. We must begin to dwell upon the infinite possibilities and potentials within our lives, rather than our limitations. When we do, we discover that we are no longer at the mercy of either our life circumstances or our bodies. We begin to discover the creative possibilities that exist within limitations.

> *I chop wood.*
> *I carry water.*
> *This is my magic.*

Within this Zen Buddhist poem is the essence of holistic healing. Everything we do within the physical, even chopping wood or carrying water, is magical. We are a spiritual essence, and we have manifested in a physical form. If we can manifest something as magnificent as this human body, then we can certainly manifest a little better health, prosperity, and joy as well.

The ways of accomplishing this are many. Some require great study and formal education. However, the techniques in this book can be used by anyone. Even those who know nothing of metaphysics or music will find success with the techniques described. These techniques are not complicated, mystical, or beyond ordinary comprehension.

Through simple sound and music therapies, each of us can add a little more light, energy, and health into our lives and the lives of those we touch. That is the wonder of healing—that is the wonder of the human being! And it is to this discovery that the methods in this handbook will lead.

The only pain that is easy to endure
is someone else's.

Anonymous French Philosopher

Chapter 2

Simple Sound Healing Tools

In the last months of my father's life, the pain from his cancer grew worse. The cancer had moved into his spine and he had trouble moving, bending, and in general getting about. The pain had become intense.

Upon a visit with him several months before he died, he allowed me to use some sound techniques on his pain. When I finished, his pain was diminished greatly and he was able to bend and move around with an ease that he had not experienced in some time.

He enjoyed this for about an hour or two and then lost his temper over a trivial matter with my sister—how best to hang a picture. Within five minutes, he was complaining about the pain once more.

Take time to remember that as we go about our activities, the effects will continue to stay with us and will build only if WE ALLOW THEM TO.

Music and sound affect us on multiple levels. Learning to apply music to produce a change in various conditions—physical and psychological—is not difficult.

Most sound and music therapies are easily applied by anyone, but music therapy is an active process. It is more than just listening to some music and "being healed." Listening passively will help, but the effects are not nearly as beneficial or long lasting as they are if we make a concerted effort to consciously enjoy and reinforce the process.

No special knowledge or prior training is essential. We do not need to play a musical instrument. We do not need to be schooled in music theory. In fact, weeding through all of the theory is time consuming and frequently an anesthetic for the brain. The techniques provided in this handbook are effective whether we have musical training or not. With just a little awareness, we each can use musical rhythms, tones, instruments, compositions, and vocalizations to interact with our different physical and psychological conditions.

All aspects of the healing field, traditional and non-traditional, serve a purpose. It is not the intent of this book to give one credence over another. The techniques provided serve a two-fold purpose:

1. To reveal that there are alternatives available (music being one), and
2. To provide simple tools in sound therapy for the average person, so that he or she can experience that effectiveness and thus enable greater participation in one's own health maintenance.

There are many ways of healing—many ways of restoring and maintaining balance. We each have our own unique energy system, and thus we each must work to find the method or combination of methods that works best for us as individuals. These techniques are those I have found helpful for myself and in my own healing work with others. They are methods that have been used in some form by therapists and others within the medical and healing field.

As you learn of these guidelines, reshape them into methods that work best for you. Remember that when music sounds good to us, it is an audible signal that the music IS good for us! We must trust what sounds good to our ears. And then we must build upon that.

General Guidelines and Helpful Hints

When using any healing technique, it is always best to assume a comfortable position. This can be a seated or prone position. Some individuals use a reclining chair, some the floor, and others use a massage table. Use what you have available and what is comfortable for you.

At times, it is appropriate to experience healing music while performing other activities: while doing daily chores, while at work, while doing something

creative. With some applications of sound healing, we can easily go about our business with the healing music playing in the background. Even then, the background music and the sound vibrations will still affect us. When we bring our full attention to the music, the effects are even greater.

Music therapy is an active process. It is not just a matter of listening to some music and "being healed." Listening passively will help, but the music's effects are more beneficial and longer lasting when we make a concerted effort to consciously enjoy and reinforce the process.

Music is a powerful healing tool, but so is silence. We must also embrace silence. I once heard that silence is the womb out of which sound is born. We live in a society permeated by sound and noise. Occasionally the best thing we can do is to use moments of silence to replenish ourselves. A moment of silence is especially helpful prior to each session or application of sound therapy. In this way, the healing music we employ is born anew out of that womb of silence, and its impact upon us is heightened.

Remember to use the imaginative faculty of the brain. Maintain the proper state of mind throughout the process. Keep in mind: "All energy follows thought!" Where we put out thoughts, that is where the energy will flow.

Experiment. Find the method or combination of methods that work best for you. For some people, focusing on only one technique will work best. Others may find combining them more effective. This is why a variety of techniques are presented.

Music Basics

The following information about the Western musical scale is all you need to know to create a stable foundation for working with music therapy.

The Western muscial scale is based upon eight successive tones, or an *octave*. The first note of an octave is called its *key note, tonic,* or *dominant*. Counting upward, this note is followed by the *second, third, fourth,* and so on. The eighth full step up is the same tone as the key note—only higher pitched. It completes the octave, the musical scale most people know as "*do, re, me fa, sol, la ti, do*."

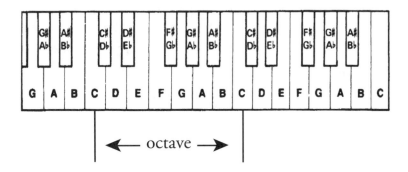

The Western world uses the generic scale of middle C, the note of C closest to the middle of the piano keyboard, as its primary reference point for all other octaves. The interval between the dominant or first note and the same note eight full steps higher or lower is called a *perfect octave.*

Each step or note within that octave is an important tone for a specific system of the body and its organs. Thus, we can use the musical scale to balance the entire body.

A Sample Healing Session

A good healing session rarely takes more than an hour. It is better to do shorter sessions frequently than a few long sessions. A good rule of thumb when it comes to any therapy is that a little can go a long way. Ten to thirty minutes, once or twice a day, is more than sufficient. For chronic conditions, you may wish to perform several sessions in the course of the day. A session in the morning and one at night can be beneficial in strengthening particular systems of the body and in helping to prevent manifestations of chronic problems. The effects of music and sound therapy are cumulative! The more we are exposed to beneficial music, the greater the benefits.

A healing session should include the following components:

- preparation,
- experiencing the music, and
- grounding and assimilating the energy.

PREPARATION

Preparing for a healing session involves creating a peaceful environment and performing a progressive relaxation before starting.

Whenever possible, eliminate outer distractions. Take the phone off the hook, and make sure you won't be disturbed or interrupted. Make sure the room where you will be working is neat and uncluttered.

Dim the lights or use colored candles and compatible fragrances to enhance the effectiveness. Sit or lie where you can be comfortable for a half hour.

Perform a progressive relaxation. The more relaxed you are, the more beneficial the session will be and the greater the effects of the music.

1. Focus quiet attention on each part of the body.
2. Visualize and send warm, soothing energies to each part of the body.
3. Starting with the feet and moving up to the top of the head (or vice versa), breathe deeply, smoothly, and easily.

Don't focus on work, your family, or anything outside of your own comfort and your own healing.

EXPERIENCING THE MUSIC

In music therapy, we want the music to embrace and flow over us. We should allow ourselves to truly experience the music. Remember to use the imaginative faculty of the brain.

Keep in mind: "All energy follows thought!" Where we put our thoughts, there the energy will flow. To further your experience with the music, keep two things in mind:

1. Play the music at a comfortable volume.
2. Give yourself up to the music.

Setting the volume too low is much better than setting it too high. As you relax, you will become more sound sensitive, so what may seem a bit too low in the beginning may be just right as you relax.

If you can hold a quiet conversation easily against the background of the music, you have found an effective volume.

Giving yourself up to the music means visualizing the music's working upon your body, affecting the appropriate system, balancing and strengthening it.

Don't try to analyze and control the music. As the music plays, see and feel it surrounding you,

embracing you, passing through you, filling you. Listen, see, feel, and imagine the sounds encircling you, flowing through you, and filling you.

Visualize yourself taking in the sound, absorbing it with each breath. Visualize and feel it balancing and strengthening your body. Feel it releasing stress and tension throughout the body.

Don't be concerned if the music stimulates your imagination and don't worry if you fall asleep. Both of these reactions signal the release of stress.

Grounding and Assimilating the Energy

When the music ends, remain still for several minutes. If your eyes have been closed, open them slowly and allow them to adjust to the light. Perform a slow stretch of each major body part. Feel how good it is to stretch when you are relaxed. Don't be in a rush to get up.

Take your time and absorb the energies. Don't jump up immediately, run around, and involve yourself in hectic activities. Just sit quietly for five minutes or so and enjoy how relaxed and strengthened you feel. You may even wish to offer a prayer of thanks for the blessing of this music healing. When you do get up, remember that the healing benefits will build as the day progresses and as we repeat the therapy.

Changing Your Healing Sessions

Sometimes you will think it necessary to change a particular technique you have been using. This is a positive sign. It reflects you are changing as your body responds to the therapy. In time, you will come to trust what feels right for you.

If a piece of music or a particular therapy sounds good to you, use it. This is an audible clue that it will be beneficial for you. Honor all of your responses.

Four Primary Tools of Music Therapy

Most techniques for sound and music therapy require no formal training. Some of the methods that follow require little active participation, but the more we participate actively in the process, the greater will be the benefits.

MUSICAL TOOL #1:
MUSIC AND RHYTHM STYLES

Different styles of music and their rhythms have beneficial effects upon different systems and organs of the body. Listening to various styles of music and rhythm is a means of balancing the functions of the body. For example, Baroque music is soothing and strengthening to the heart rhythms and circulatory system. Rhapsodies are strengthening to the muscular system and stimulating to the nervous system. Waltz rhythms are beneficial to emotional health, mental stress, and digestion.

Classical music can be a wonderful tool for balancing and healing. Different systems and organs of the body are more responsive to specific musical keys. Listening to classical compositions written in a particular musical key, rhythm, and style subtly and positively impacts functions of corresponding body systems and its organs.

Most libraries contain listings of classical compositions within their card catalogues and computers, along with the musical key in which they were written. Thus we can easily find and use music that can benefit us. Specific classical music compositions and their appropriate musical key are provided in the chapter corresponding to each major system of the body.

We can heighten the effects of the styles and rhythms of music by listening to them to in a meditative state. In fact, by eliminating as many outside distractions as possible, we can enhance all of the effects of music therapy. Even if we only use them as background music for daily activities, they will assist in correcting imbalances related to specific systems of the body.

MUSICAL TOOL #2:
TONAL & INSTRUMENTAL HEALING

Different musical instruments will also influence the human energy system. Ninety percent of the body's activities are controlled and mediated by the subconscious mind, but there are many levels to the subconscious mind. Different levels direct and mediate the functions of different systems, organs, and activities within the body, responding more strongly to different musical tones, rhythms, vocalizations, instrumentation, movements, and so on.

We can thus use music and sounds to act upon specific levels of the subconscious mind, thereby balancing and strengthening their corresponding system and organs. For example, flutes and woodwinds will affect the level of the subconscious mind that directs left hemisphere activity of the brain and the activities of the digestive system. Harp music is soothing to the circulatory system, while violins can ease nervous conditions by acting upon the level of the subconscious linked to it.

For each bodily system and its corresponding organs, the musical instruments beneficial for them are listed, along with appropriate specific instrumental compositions. Simply listening to these pieces of music and instruments regularly or as background music will help balance and strengthen the corresponding systems and organs.

These musical compositions and instruments can be incorporated with the classical healing technique described in Musical Therapy Tool #1. By combining a classical piece of music in the appropriate style and in the appropriate musical key, we greatly amplify the effects.

On the following page you will find information about the Eastern chakra tradition for the various systems of the body. In Eastern traditions, chakras are "centers of activity for the reception, assimilation and transmission of life energies."[1] In the East, there are many references to chakras or energy centers associated with the body.

One of the easiest ways to understand the chakras is to think of them as reflecting specific levels of the subconscious mind without respect to the physical location in the body. It is most important to remember that each of these centers (and the systems and organs of the body they mediate and direct) is more likely to respond to specific tones, rhythms, and instruments.

In keeping with my promise to focus upon practical application, only as much theory as is necessary to begin work with these applications is

---

[1] Anodea Judith, *Wheels of Life* (St. Paul: Llewellyn Publications, 1987), p. 1.

Theory of the Chakras

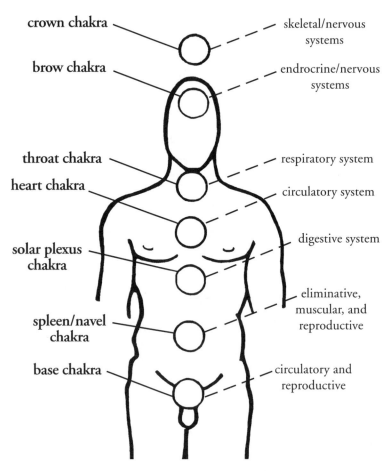

crown chakra — skeletal/nervous systems

brow chakra — endrocrine/nervous systems

throat chakra — respiratory system

heart chakra — circulatory system

solar plexus chakra — digestive system

spleen/navel chakra — eliminative, muscular, and reproductive

base chakra — circulatory and reproductive

The chakras mediate all energy within the body.
Although reflected in the physical body, they relate most strongly
to specific levels of the subconscious mind, each individual level
controlling and directing specific systems and organs.

provided. For more detailed information about chakras, you might want to refer to *The Healer's Manual: A Beginner's Guide to Vibrational Therapies* and other books on this topic listed in the bibliography.

MUSICAL TOOL #3:
VOCAL REMEDIES

Three common forms of vocal remedies are *toning, chanting,* and *affirming.* Toning, chanting, and affirming are processes of vibrating sounds, tones, and words of power to assist in the healing process. They are cleansing, harmonizing, and healing and can be used to restore homeostasis (balance) to various systems.

Voice releases power in the direction of our thoughts, thereby sending energy to an appropriate area of the body. We can use vocal sounds to balance the entire physiological system or only one particular area of the body.

Performing vocal remedies is simple and can be used with vowel tones, mantras, and words of power. Begin by reviewing which tones, mantras, or words

of power are beneficial for the organ or system you wish to influence. Each chapter on bodily systems contains selected musical compositions, tones, sounds,

words of power, and affirmations beneficial to that system.

Once you have selected the vocal expression you wish to use, perform them in a seated, prone, or standing position. A simple ten minutes of these remedies once or twice a day can be a wonderful healing tonic. People are often amazed how simple and yet how powerfully effective these remedies are.

Toning

Toning is the first vocal remedy to learn, as chanting and affirming are simply distinct variations of toning. Toning releases sounds in a manner that directs the vocal energy to the corresponding system of the body. Vowel sounds are some of the easiest to use when beginning to use toning.

Toning begins with focus upon a particular system or area of the body. If toning for yourself, simply focus on the corresponding body part, which will direct the sound energy to that area. If performing toning for another person, focus upon that area of the other person's body and visualize the sound issuing out from you to balance the appropriate part of the other person's body.

Once you have determined the vowel sound, mantram, or affirmation appropriate for the vocal remedy, use the following steps:

1. Slowly inhale, toning the sound silently. Hold the sound and the breath. Then, slowly exhale, sounding the tone audibly.

   Allow the voice to find its own pitch, volume, and length.

2. Repeat this sequence. In, silent. Out, audible. In. Out. Silent. Audible. Spiritual. Physical. This is the dynamic of sacred sound.

   Find the rhythm that is comfortable for you.

To enhance the effects, tone in the appropriate musical key. For example, if working upon the heart or circulatory parts of the body, use the long A (*ay*) sound. By toning in the key of F or F sharp, the effects will be enhanced. To help with musical key, you may wish to purchase an inexpensive pitch pipe.

Chanting

Chanting is a second form of vocal music therapy and is actually a form of toning. Chanting, or repeating various syllables and affirmations, can be used to stimulate both physiological and psychological changes. Mantras and words of power come in many types and from many different traditions. A little experimentation will help find those that feel most comfortable to us. Every syllable or word should be given equal emphasis in the toning and chanting process.

Pay attention to your voice as you tone. It will provide audible clues as to the success of the toning and chanting by responding as a kind of echo location. Cracking and wavering of the voice during the toning process reflects imbalance. Continue the toning and chanting until the voice smooths, an audible clue that the toning is working.

After concentrated toning or chanting for a specific condition, it is also beneficial to tone briefly for each of the systems or chakras to reinforce the entire body's physiological processes. To be effective, use several repetitions of each sound for each of the systems of the body. This is a wonderful way of maintaining and restoring daily balance.

Affirming

Affirming is a way of speaking to ourselves to elicit specific effects. As we discussed earlier, certain emotions and mental attitudes can aggravate and even create physical health imbalances because the subconscious mind takes what we say and think in a literal manner. We tell ourselves we get two colds every winter, and the subconscious mind immediately begins working with the body's energies. As winter approaches, it has stimulated enough changes so that we are more susceptible to "catching" those two colds.

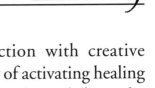

Affirmations, in conjunction with creative visualization, are a dynamic way of activating healing energies within us. All sounds and words have the capability of affecting us. Affirmations that are spoken, chanted, and sung are the most powerful. We can use affirmations as positive, vocal statements to release emotional and mental issues that may be aggravating a particular condition in the body.

An even more effective way of using affirmations is to create our own. This is not a difficult process. We begin by determining the quality we wish to affirm. We should always phrase the affirmation in the present tense. We live in an ever-present moment, thus it is always beneficial to begin the affirmation with the "I am…" phrase, such as "I am joyful and full of life!" The shorter, simpler, and more explicit the affirmation, the more effective it is. The sample affirmations provided for each major system of the body are simply a starting point. Don't be limited to them. Expand on them and make them your own.

Affirmation Toning with Breath

Once the affirmation is chosen or created, tone it with feeling in the same manner described earlier. Combine the affirmation toning with breathing.

1. Inhale, and as you inhale, sound the affirmation silently.
2. Hold the breath briefly.
3. Exhale, sounding the affirmation audibly.

While performing the affirmation, it is helpful to visualize its essence and impact. This creates the feeling of belief and heightens the effect upon the body.

AFFIRMATION TONING TO BACKGROUND MUSIC

To enhance the effects even further, combine the affirmation with music appropriate to the system being worked on. For example, if using an affirmation to strengthen the heart, perform the affirmation to music composed in the key of F or in the Baroque style to strengthen cardiovascular rhythms.

Play the music softly in the background. Take a few moments to relax comfortably. The more relaxed you are, the more effective the affirmation will be.

1. Relax. As you relax, begin breathing in a slow, rhythmic manner.
2. Inhale and speak the affirmation silently.
3. Hold your breath briefly, imagining and feeling the energy of it awakening and stimulating the entire bodily system.
4. Exhale, speaking the affirmation audibly. Try to imagine and feel its full impact. If the affirmation involves "joy," try and feel joyful.

Affirmations do not have to be repeated thousands of times. An affirmation spoken with the proper visualization and feeling behind it will be much more effective than one repeatedly chanted without feeling. The right affirmation, combined with the appropriate visualization, emotion, and belief, can have a dynamic effect. In fact, ten minutes of a good affirmation, accompanied by the proper music, will bring a change in your overall mood, and this is a signal that the process is working. For those times when we feel particularly stressed, it can be beneficial to use the affirmations periodically throughout the day.

MUSICAL TOOL #4:
MUSIC AND MOVEMENT

One of the most powerful ways of using music and sound to heal is in conjunction with physical movement. Movement and dance, like sound and music, are universal.

Physical movement helps the healing sounds manifest more dynamically within the human body. The central nervous system and the neurological systems transform musical tones and rhythms into movement patterns. Movement and dance actualize energy. Different movements will activate energies and forces, external to the body and internally as well.

Movement is basic to the functions of the body. Various movements, postures, gestures, and exercises—when combined with the right music—will accelerate the strengthening and healing of the body's systems and organs. Dance therapy, the applications of movement to healing, is a tremendous support to music therapy. Each reinforces the other. I have included simple and effective physical movements that are beneficial and supportive of the music therapies for each of the systems of the body.

The process for combining the movements with the music is simple. We should always begin by taking a few moments to relax and stretch. Although the movements provided are not intense, if we are not used to movement, we may not feel comfortable. The movements provided should only be performed to the degree that we are comfortable.

Try to keep the movements simple and fluid. Allow for your own individual expression and adaptation. Try not be critical of your ability with the movements. It is not the quality of the performance, but the participation in the movement that invokes and activates the energy. As you work with the movements, they will become easier. The more frequently they are used with the corresponding music, the more energy is released into and for the benefit of the appropriate bodily systems and organs.

Complimentary Music Therapy Tools

There are many holistic modalities. A number of them are complimentary to sound and music therapies, increasing their overall effectiveness. They also provide a means of working more independently on a daily basis to establish and restore balance. Our body is changing constantly, and thus the modalities used to establish balance may have to be changed and adapted periodically. Complimentary modalities can assist us in this process.

For each system of the body, there is a list of complimentary healing modalities for those who may wish to experiment with other holistic methods. In other words, for each system of the body, its organs and the specific conditions, there are not only the sound therapies but also colors and fragrances that are compatible. This means you will have the key information you need to begin working with color and aroma therapies in conjunction with the sound and music. For example, flute music can be combined with the color yellow and peppermint fragrance to help ease indigestion.

Color and fragrance, like sound and music, have the ability to touch us on multiple levels. Everyone is affected by color more often than we may realize.

Although this book is not designed to teach all of the significance of various colors and fragrances, it will provide some basic guidelines.[2]

COLOR THERAPIES

There are three simple ways of using color therapy to compliment music therapy: through color breath, with colored swatches, and with colored candles.

Color Breathing

During the musical therapy session, color breathing can be employed.

1. Visualize yourself breathing in and filling the body with the complimentary color(s).
2. Imagine the color filling the body and alleviating the condition.

Color Swatches

Use colored swatches or material throughout the musical healing session. This can be as simple as holding a piece of cloth of the appropriate color over the area of the body needing balance.

You can also wrap your body in an appropriately colored cloth throughout the session. The body will

[2] For more detailed information and applications on color and aroma therapy, you might want to refer to my *How to Heal with Color* and *The Healer's Manual* .

absorb the color vibrations, especially when they are compatible with the music being used.

Colored Candles

Burn a candle of the appropriate color within the area in which the healing session is taking place. As the candle burns, the color vibration is released into the air and absorbed by the body to reinforce the effects of the healing sounds.

Aromatherapy

When it comes to aromatherapy, essential oils are most beneficial. Although incense can be effective, essential oils, through the distilling process, will have a much more potent effect.

As with color healing, there are three simple ways of using aromatherapy to compliment and amplify the music therapy: in diluted forms, in a bath, and as a room fragrance.

In Diluted Forms

The oils can be used like a perfume in a diluted form. Essential oils are created through a distilling process and thus they can be irritating to the skin; hence, dilution is important. When diluted, a small amount can be massaged into the area being focused upon through the healing session.

Ted Andrews   55

In a Bath

The oils can also be used in a bath prior to the actual music therapy session. Half of a capful of essential oil within the bath can be a powerful healing tool. Listening to the appropriate music while soaking in a hot tub with the appropriate fragrance is a magnificent way to relax and thus heal ourselves.

As a Room Fragrance

The fragrance can also be used in several ways to permeate the room in which the music therapy is going to occur. This can be done in several ways. The oil can be placed within vaporizers, diffusers, or potpourri pots, or a drop or two of the oil can be placed in a small bowl of water. The fragrance will permeate the room in which the music therapy will occur and thus amplify the effects.

Do not be afraid to experiment with these complimentary modalities or others in combination with the music therapy. At different times, some may be more effective for you than others. These complimentary therapies are suggestions, and they simply help us in participating even more fully in the healing process.

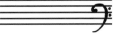

ORGANS IDENTIFIED BY BODILY SYSTEM

The therapies discussed in the following chapters are organized by bodily system. The following table indicates which organs are associated with which bodily systems. Appendix C provides a quick reference guide to various imbalances and their complimentary therapies. Appendix E provides a list of health problems related to the physical systems as discussed by chapter in this book.

ORGAN	CIRCULATORY	DIGESTIVE	ELIMINATION	GLANDULAR	NERVOUS	REPRODUCTIVE	RESPIRATORY
arteries	x						x
bladder			x				
brain					x		
cerebellum					x		
diaphragm		x					
esophagus	x						x
heart	x						
kidneys			x				
liver		x					
lungs							x
mouth		x					x
nerves					x		
ovaries						x	
pancreas		x		x			
small intestine		x					
spinal cord					x		
testes				x			x
thyroid				x			

*Energy is a dynamic force, in constant flux, which
circulates throughout the body.*[1]

---

[1] Dr. Stephen T. Chang, *The Complete System of Self-Healing* (San
Francisco: Tao Publishing, 1986), p. 37.

Chapter 3

Music Therapies for Circulation

The circulatory system is the body's transportation system, moving blood throughout the body to supply cells with nutrients and to remove their wastes. The circulatory system is comprised of three major aspects: a pump to circulate the fluids (heart), the fluid to circulate nutrients (blood), and the vessels to contain the fluids (arteries, veins, and capillaries).

The Circulatory System

The *heart*, a muscular pump about the size of our fist, is the primary organ of the circulatory system. As the strongest muscle in the human body, the heart beats an average of 70 times per minute and 38 million times each year. In the course of a day, the heart pumps between four and five thousand gallons of blood. The heart is actually a double pump with blood circulating in the form of a figure eight. The right side of the heart receives blood from the body and pumps it to the lungs. The left side receives blood from the lungs and pumps it to the body.

The *blood* is the link between our body cells and the outer world. The foods we eat and the air we breathe are the parts of our outer environment that come into contact with the blood. Blood transports those parts of the outer world environment through our internal environment. The transport items between worlds include food, vitamins, water, minerals, oxygen and such that are necessary for living cells.

The blood serves five main functions:

- transports nutrients and wastes,
- helps regulate fluids in other body compartments,

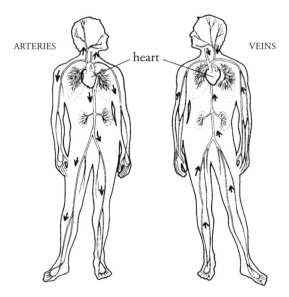

- buffers and protects us against toxins through antibodies within the bloodstream,
- helps regulate body temperature, and
- prevents loss of blood through its ability to coagulate.

The *blood vessels*, the arteries, veins, and capillaries, are the modes of transportation for the blood: "If our blood vessels were placed end to end, they would reach the astounding length of nearly 100,000 miles!"[2] The *arteries* carry blood from the heart toward the tissues in the body. They play an important role in the regulation of blood pressure and blood flow. The *veins* carry blood toward the heart, away from the tissues. The *capillaries* transport blood to the tissues, organs, and individual cells. Their job is to assist in the exchange of materials between blood and cells.

Cardiovascular Problems

Millions of people suffer annually from cardiovascular problems—some disorder of the heart and blood vessels. Problems with circulation are most frequently tied to issues surrounding how we handle

---

[2] James Otto, *Modern Health* (New York: Holt, Rhinehart & Winston, Inc., 1971), p. 442.

emotions. Certain emotions and attitudes are more likely to create stress and imbalances within the circulatory system, especially in cardiovascular areas.

When circulatory problems arise within our life, we need to examine how we are handling our emotions. Frequently problems can stem from some lack of vitality and movement within our emotional life.

Problems can also arise from excessive or inappropriate expression in some avenue of our emotional life. When expressed too freely and without control, we can dissipate our vitality, creating low blood pressure. When we do not allow our emotions proper expression, they will build internally, often resulting in high blood pressure.

Certain emotions and mental attitudes strongly effect the circulatory system. The twelve most common of these are the following:

- anger,
- insecurity,
- possessiveness,
- self-doubt,
- mistrust,
- needing recognition,
- lack of will,
- miserliness,

- not expressing emotions,
- inappropriate expressions of emotions,
- failure to move forward, and
- trying to do too much too soon.

As with any health problem, there can be a variety of hidden issues influencing a condition or making us more susceptible to imbalances. Should a problem arise with any general area of circulation, a little self-examination may help to clarify the issues contributing to the condition.

The following questions are good to ask for any problem associated with circulation:

Are we becoming locked in the past and afraid to move on?

Are we not resolving old, emotional issues?

Are we refusing to make the moves in life that we should?

Do we need a fresh course of action?

Are we growing or are we feeling stifled?

Are we trying to force growth and movement?

Are we harboring feelings of self-defeatism?

Are we going in too many directions at once, scattering our energies?

Music Therapies for Circulation

1. THERAPEUTIC MUSIC AND RHYTHM STYLES

 Baroque and Renaissance music can be very beneficial for heart and circulatory systems. Classical music, including marches, can also be used to stimulate the heart.

Baroque Music

Baroque music is the most basic and therapeutic kind of music that can best benefit the circulatory system. It can be used effectively for any circulatory stress, imbalance or problem, strengthening the entire system.

The Baroque period began just before 1600 and lasted until 1750. This period has strongly affected many of our modern expressions of music. Here we find the beginnings of our modern opera and ballet, and most forms of instrumental music: sonata, concerto, fugue, toccata, and such.

During this time, harmonic theory and the figured bass came into play. This becomes especially significant from a metaphysical perspective, when we consider that the heart chakra has the greatest connection to overall body harmony. The base chakra,

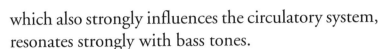

which also strongly influences the circulatory system, resonates strongly with bass tones.

The violin family reached its highest development during Baroque times, and many Baroque violin concertos are beneficial to the body's circulatory rhythms. String instruments are beneficial to the heart and all of its functions. Today, Baroque music is frequently being played in the background during cardiac surgery to facilitate the normal heart rhythms, thus decreasing bleeding and accelerating healing.

Baroque composers (such as Bach, Handel, and Vivaldi) wanted their music to be extremely expressive, to deal with the passionate emotions or the "affections." These included such emotions as pain, sorrow, love, devotion, all of which strongly affect the heart and the circulatory system. For example, the Baroque cantatas joined instruments and voices to illustrate devotional texts. Baroque cantatas can be very detoxifying to negative emotional states. Using them as background music will help clean the air in a room where strong emotions have been expressed, such as after arguments or fights.

Some of the more beneficial Baroque composers to listen to for circulatory conditions are Bach, Handel and Vivaldi. See the table on the following page for details.

BAROQUE MUSIC FOR THE CIRCULATORY SYSTEM

Composer	Work	Effect
Bach	Brandenburg Concertos no. 1 and no. 2 in F Major	strengthens the heart and the heart rhythms
	Fugue and Toccata in D Minor	releases the flow of emotions
	Contatas	cleanses highly charged emotional states
Handel	Water Music	ensures the proper flow and circulation blocked by emotions
	Harp Concerto	calms anger and high pressure conditions
Vivaldi	The Four Seasons	balances the flow of elements throughout the body and through the blood vessels

Renaissance Music

Renaissance music and rhythms are also beneficial for the heart and circulatory system because they are very soothing to emotional states. Many of the Baroque rhythms and styles evolved out of the Renaissance period of music in Europe.

When my father passed away, he and my mother were living in South Carolina. My brothers and I drove down for one of two services that would be held for him. Throughout the day, the emotions would periodically and understandably run high. I played a piece of Renaissance music on my mother's stereo, and the emotional level of those people present would drop in intensity. When the tape finished, the emotions would again start to rise.

Noticing this, I thought, "What a wonderful time to experiment!" Throughout the day, I would watch the rise and fall of emotions against the music of the tape I was playing. When the emotions started to rise, I would play the tape again softly in the background. The emotional level would then calm down. When the tape played out, I would not turn it back on immediately, and the emotions would run high again. When that occurred, I would start the tape over.

It was truly amazing watching the response the music had upon the emotional levels of those present.

Dance of the Renaissance and *Dream of the Troubadours* by Richard Searles and Gilber Yslas (Sundown Records) are beneficial modern pieces in the Renaissance rhythm and style.

Marches and Classical Music

Many classical compositions can be soothing and powerful while greatly influencing the physical and metaphysical circulation. Marches can be a tremendous stimulus to the circulatory system, strengthening and stabilizing it. Marches stimulate movement by awakening the courage to express. Verdi's *Triumphal March* is particularly effective because the strong march rhythms strengthen and stabilize heart and circulatory rhythms.

For any march music or compositions with strong rhythms, it is important not to listen to them too often or for too long a period. Doing so can over stimulate the body, creating tiredness and even aggravating the condition more. Ten to thirty mintues, once or twice a day is more than sufficient.

Classical Music for the Circulatory System

Composer	Work	Effect
Schubert	C Major Symphony	strengthens and stabilizes all aspects of circulatory system
Beethoven	Symphony no. 6 in F Major (Pastorale)	frees emotions, which may be hindering circulation; soothes aching hearts; opens, strengthens blood vessels
Debussy	Claire de Lune	opens flow of emotions; balances flow of body fluids; soothes entire circulatory system, including high blood pressure

2. TONAL AND INSTRUMENTAL THERAPIES

Two of the traditional chakras (the base and heart chakras) are associated with the circulatory system. The chakras are outer reflections of specific levels within the subconscious mind that control different physiological functions. Certain tones and musical keys, along with specific instruments, have a stronger impact upon the various levels of the subconscious mind, with an ability to therefore stimulate and balance their corresponding biological functions.

The Base Chakra

The *base chakra* is tied to that level of the subconscious mind, which controls general circulatory functions, particularly in the lower extremities. We can stimulate the base chakra to improve such conditions as poor circulation, anemia, varicose veins, and low blood pressure. To maximize the benefits, use music in the key of C, including C minor and C sharp, major and minor. You can also use the key note or base tone of your personal musical scale (refer to Appendix B for the musical scales for each sign of the zodiac and their corresponding chakras).

An octave of key notes can also elicit a feeling of rest and balance when played musically. Composers sometimes use an octave to elicit feelings of new wholeness; this has this same effect upon the circulatory system and helps to stabilize circulation.

All marches and music with strong steady rhythms and lots of brass and percussion instrumentation can be beneficial as well to the base chakra and the circulatory system. African style percussions are strengthening and beneficial for this, as are the "walking rhythms" of early jazz, boogie-woogie, and rock-n-roll. If we want a general pick-me-up (energy-wise), select a piece of music with a steady rhythm in bass tones.

The Heart Chakra

The *heart chakra* is linked to that level of the subconscious mind, directing cardiac functions and influencing arterial aspects of the circulatory system. Here it is helpful to use music in the key of F, including F minor and F sharp, major and minor, if you are using the generic scale of middle C. For a greater effect, use music in the natural fourth of a more personal musical scale, such as that of your own astrological sign. (Refer to Appendix B.)

Composers use the natural fourth to reflect newness, to create a sense of movement and entrance. For this reason, the fourth can be beneficial, especially after cardiac problems or cardiac surgery. Selecting compositions with stringed instruments such as harps, dulcimers, acoustic guitars, flutes, and violins will further enhance the healing aspects.

The musical selections shown in the table on the following page are beneficial to the corresponding chakra and thus assist in the healing and balancing of the circulatory system. Remember to visualize the music surrounding you and then flowing into you through the chakra. See and feel the music filling you and balancing the corresponding system.

3. VOCAL REMEDIES FOR CIRCULATION

We can use individual tones to interact with the physiological processes of the body. The human voice is our most creative instrument. We can use our voice to make others feel as if they are standing next to the divine or use our voice to make others feel wish for the end of life.

Toning

Voice has a tremendous capacity for healing. There are a variety of vocalizations that can be beneficial to the various systems and organs of the body. Two of the most effective are vowel sounds and eastern mantras. Remember that vocal sounds have the capacity to stimulate particular systems and organs of the body. In the previous chapter, we discussed the process of toning that enables this to occur. It would be beneficial to go back at this point and review this process.

The following vowel sounds and mantras are most beneficial for the circulatory system:

Chakra	Vowel Sound	Mantram
BASE	long u (*oo*)	lam (*lahm*)
HEART	long a (*ay*)	yam (*yahm*)

For the greatest effect upon the circulatory system, I recommend toning the sounds for both chakras. Some prefer to use only the vowel sounds; some prefer the mantras. Some will use both. Experiment. Find what sounds, feels, and works best for you.

To enhance the effects, tone them in the appropriate musical key. To do this, have a pitch pipe or a tuning fork available. For the base chakra sounds, use the tone of middle C or the dominant tone of your personal musical scale as reflected by your astrological sign (see Appendix B). Those born under the sign of Cancer would use the scale and the key tone of E flat. For the heart chakra, the sounds would be toned

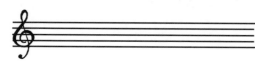

in F or in the fourth of the appropriate musical scale. For Cancerians, the tone would be an A flat, which is the fourth in the musical scale of E flat.

You might also find it beneficial to perform the toning for a specific condition while playing a piece of classical music softly in the background. By combining these therapies, you increase their effectiveness. For the circulatory system, performing the toning or chanting to Beethoven's *Symphony no. 6* can be extremely beneficial.

When toning and chanting, the effects are often felt more quickly. This is primarily because the voice is our most creative instrument. Toning enables us to use this instrument more actively in working with the particular condition. Because of this, toning rarely needs to be performed longer than ten minutes at a time and no more often than twice a day to experience wonderful results.

Affirmations Beneficial to Circulatory System

Sample affirmations beneficial to the circulatory system are listed below. You can use these or create your own. Most people find it more beneficial to create their own affirmations, particularly if they have determined the metaphysical or hidden issues affecting the condition. In creating the affirmations, examine the emotional issues that can aggravate a

**Music for the
Base and Heart Chakras**

Chakra	Composer	Work
BASE	Brahms	Symphony no. 1 in C Minor
key of C, including C minor and C sharp, major and minor	Beethoven	Fifth Symphony
	Wagner	Ride of the Valkyries
all marches	Vivaldi	Mandolin Concerto in C
HEART	Bach	Brandenburg Concertos no. 1 and no. 2
key of F, including F minor and F sharp, major and minor	Beethoven	Symphony no. 6 (Pastorale)
	Gluck	Dance of the Blessed Spirits
	Wood	Harp of Brandiswhiere
	Ladysmith Black Mambazo	most compositions

particular condition, and then create the affirmation to counteract the negative emotion.

For example, if anger is an issue creating heart problems, use opposite words to counter the anger, such as: "I am at peace. My life flows smoothly." When saying the affirmations, try to remember that the role and function of the circulatory system has to do with flow and movement.

I am in the joyful flow of life!

I am open to the flow of life!

I am at peace within the flow of life.

I am at peace and my life is balanced!

Life is balanced, joyful and free flowing!

I am at peace in the heart of activity!

I am vital and joyful in life!

You can make these affirmations even more beneficial when you ground them internally by incorporating movement. As you recite your affirmation, use The Sun Salutation described in the next section. This series of yoga exercises will greatly heighten the impact and effectiveness of your voice and the affirmation you are speaking.

WORDS OF POWER

Shaddai El Chai
shah-dye-ehl-kye

"The Almighty Living God"

This is an old Hebrew name of God representing that aspect of the Divine that exists in the flow and tides of all things in life. Thus it has connections to the flow and tides of the blood and circulatory system within humans.

Jehoval Aloah Va Daath
yah-hoh-vah-ay-loh-ah-vuh-dawth

"Divine Made Manifest in the Heart of the Mind"

This is the Hebrew name for that aspect of the Divine that serves to manifest all things in life. The mind is at the heart of all that manifests, and thus this is a name that can be chanted or toned to counter the effects that negative thinking has upon our overall health.

Raphael
rah-fah-ehl

"Angel of Beauty, Brightness, and Healing"

Sandalphon
san-dahl-fon

"Angel of Prayers and Approach"

4. MUSIC AND MOVEMENT THERAPIES

A yoga sequence can be used to stimulate and balance the heart and all circulatory rhythms. The best yoga sequence I know for this is called the *Sun Salutation*, and it can be performed to any Baroque or Renaissance piece to amplify the healing effects.

The following musical pieces are suggested for use with this exercise: *Dance of the Renaissance* by Seales and Yslas, *Pastorale* by Beethoven, *Water Music* by Handel, and *The Brandenburg Concerto* by Bach.

Do not worry if you cannot perform the exercise as described. Do the best you can knowing that whatever you do will enhance the effect. View this as a dynamic process of combining music and dance therapy. With every movement to the music, you are restoring balance.

The series of movements included in the Sun Salutation is strengthening and healing to the primary organ of the circulatory system—the heart, our sun center. The yoga exercise forces us to pay reverence to the sun of the world and the sun within (the heart). This yoga sequence is very symbolic and yet very effective in enhancing all healing aspects of circulation.

Sun Salutation

The Sun Salutation consists of twelve basic movements—symbolic of one solar year. The series of steps must be performed twice, once for each leg.

Figure A

1. Stand facing the sun or the east, from where the sun rises. Circle your arms out and bring them into prayer position at the chest (Figure A).

   With this gesture, we honor the sacredness outside of us and within us.

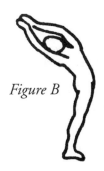

Figure B

2. Extend the arms and head up and back, looking toward the heavens and stars (Figure B). Then slowly bend forward (Figure C), bringing the hands down to the outside of the feet and touch the ground. It is not necessary to keep the legs straight. You can bend them or squat if necessary.

   This gesture reflects drawing down the light from the heavens to the earth. The heavenly light has filled your hands and passes into the earth through them.

Figure C

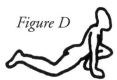

Figure D

3. Step back with the right leg (Figure D). Raise your head up, always looking toward the sun, bringing the energy into motion so you can look at the sun even more.

    As long as our face is toward the sun, there is no darkness in our life.

Figure E

4. Step back with the other foot (Figure E), supported by your own hands and feet. Don't worry if you cannot support yourself in this way; just use your knees to help.

    This movement reminds you to attain strength and support from the Higher Light, trusting and allowing it to support you and your life at times.

Figure F

5. Lower your knees and chest while lifting the buttocks into the air (Figure F).

    This position is very humbling and through it you acknowledge your own light, which no matter how great, is humbled before the Light of Lights.

6. From this position move into the traditional cobra asana of yoga (Figure G).

Figure G

Visualize yourself like a snake basking in the sun which now rises up to new health and new work.

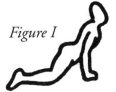

7. Your life is flowing anew, as you raise the buttocks up, experiencing new circulation (Figure H).

Figure H

8. You are energized and balanced again, as you step forward with the right leg, bringing it up between the arms. This is followed by the left leg (Figure I).

Figure I

Your life and your blood is balanced.

9. You then begin to rise up with new vitality and energy (Figure J).

Figure J

Ted Andrews

10. Then, as in the beginning, you lift yourself straight, arms overhead, your own inner sun or heart, balanced and in rhythm with that of the outer suns and nature (Figure K).

The hands are then brought to prayer position at the chest, and our circulation is balanced, strong, renewed and vital.

Figure K

This completes one half of the salutation. It should be repeated, step-by-step, but by stepping with the left leg first. This repetition can be envisioned as balancing both the arterial and venous aspects of circulation.

SUMMARY OF MUSICAL GUIDELINES
FOR CIRCULATION

Chakra	Base	Heart
TONE	C (*do*)	F (*fa*)
VOWEL	long u (*oo*)	long a (*ay*)
MANTRAM	lam	yam
INSTRUMENT	percussion, bass	harps, violins, lutes
STYLE	boogie-woogie, walking-style	Baroque, madrigal, Renaissance

Complimentary

IMBALANCE	INSTRUMENT	KEY
circulation (general)	percussion. bass	C, F
anemia	percussion	C
high blood pressure	strings, harp, violin	F
low blood pressure	percussion	C, D
heart	strings, harp	F

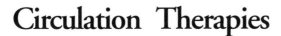

Circulation Therapies

Sounds	Colors	Aromas
(*oo, ay*)	red, green	cinnamon, rose
(*oo*)	red	cinnamon
(*ay*)	blue, green	rose, eucalyptus
(*oo, oh*)	red, orange	cinnamon, sage
(*ay*)	green, pink	rose, jasmine*

* Jasmine frequently stimulates the mucous membranes and may result in coughing up mucous throughout the night, along with stimulating sinus drainage which could interfere with sleep. Caution is advised.

Ted Andrews

85

When we eat in a healthy, harmonious way,
our ability to attune and commune
with the Divine is enhanced.[1]

---

[1] Gabriel Cousens, M.D., *Spiritual Nutrition and The Rainbow Diet* (Boulder, Colorado: Cassandra Press, 1986), p. 1.

Chapter 4

Music Therapies for Digestion

Digestion is the process of converting food to nutrients essential for the body. Every organ makes its own contribution to this step-by-step process, which may involve both mechanical and chemical actions.

The Digestive System

The digestive system has two primary functions: ingestion and absorption. Food enters the *mouth* where chewing and swallowing begin the process of breaking down the substance. Food descends from the mouth through the *esophagus* to the inner organs of the digestive system. Although the esophagus does not have a direct digestive action, it is necessary to the transport of food internally so the digestive process can occur.

From the esophagus, food travels to the *stomach* and the internal organs of digestion. Contrary to what many people believe, the stomach is not the most vital organ for digestion, although it is a primary one. The stomach serves as a reservoir for storing and

digesting food, where the stomach acid helps break the complex protein molecules into simpler forms, converting the food into nutrients.

The *small intestine* is actually the most vital organ of the digestive organs. About 1 inch in diameter and about 23 feet in length, the small intestines completely digest all three classes of foods (carbohydrates, fats, and proteins). This occurs through secretions which act on the food while within the small intestines. These secretions are from intestinal glands, the liver and the pancreas.

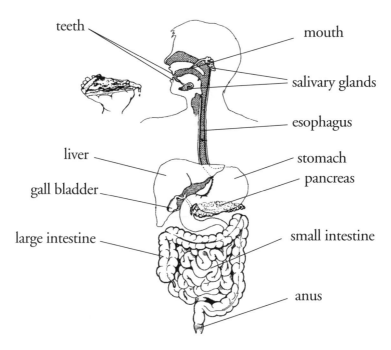

The *liver* is the largest organ in the body and serves multiple functions:

- as a storehouse for digested food, particularly carbohydrates,
- as a chemical factory for fats and amino acids,
- as a regulator of the body's blood sugar, and
- as a blood filter in both digestion and elimination.

In digestion, the *liver* secretes bile (a fluid containing various salts and other substances) essential to the digestion of fats. In elimination, the bile salts act as a detergent for the blood, enabling the kidneys to filter those particles that must be eliminated from those that can be absorbed as nutrients. Between periods of digestion, bile from the liver backs up into the *gall bladder*, where it is stored and concentrated.

The *pancreas* is actually an endocrine system gland, but it serves a vital digestive role as well. The pancreatic juices flow from cells of the pancreas and contain enzymes which act upon the carbohydrates, fats, and proteins, continuing the breakdown of the food substances so the nutrients can more easily be absorbed and used by the body.

A Healthy Digestive System

The American public spends hundreds of millions of dollars a year on laxatives, tonics, and other aids to digestion. In truth, a healthy digestive system does not require outside assistance from drugs. Such a system rarely requires more than a well-balanced diet, proper amounts of exercise, and the proper amounts of water. However, we can keep our digestive system healthier by avoiding or alleviating certain stresses in our daily lives.

Problems with the Digestive System

Any problem with the digestive system should encourage us to examine what we are taking in (ingestion) and absorbing within our lives that is inappropriate. Are we being forced to swallow things that we shouldn't? Are we refusing to take in or bite into a new experience that could be beneficial to us?

In particular, problems with the mouth and esophagus should raise questions about what kind of nourishment we are or are not taking in our daily life—both from a nutritional aspect as well as from an emotional perspective. We have all heard the phrase: "That's hard to swallow." Problems in the throat area may be exasperated or brought on by aspects of our lives that are "hard to swallow."

Problems with the gall bladder can be triggered or aggravated by trying to digest experiences in life too quickly. Gall bladder problems may also result from not digesting the life experiences we have had, perhaps holding onto them and allowing them to harden like gallstones.

Stresses, both emotional and mental, can also irritate or even create digestive system imbalances revolving around the following easily identifiable issues:

- being overly critical or overly criticized,
- being dogmatic or around those who are,
- always looking for the short and easy,
- being judgmental about yourself or others,
- bullying or being bullied,
- planning but not following through,
- needing constant change,
- feeling deprived or depriving others,
- being too meticulous, and
- being overly rigid.

If digestive problems start to surface, they can provide us with an opportunity to clarify important issues influencing our health. With a little self-

examination, we can discern the issues that may have contributed to or caused the imbalance.

On the next page I've listed some questions you might want to ask if digestive problems arise.

Are we rushing and not taking things in a step by step manner?

Are we or someone around us being too critical?

Are we finding it difficult to let go of the old issues?

Are we holding onto the past rather than moving forward?

Who or what are we taking into our life that we shouldn't?

Are we allowing what others do and say to eat at us?

Are we not taking in the new that is presenting itself to us?

Are we feeling deprived on any level?

Are we or others around us being too judgmental?

Are we feeling isolated?

Are we using what is available to us or is it being wasted?

Are we insulating and isolating ourselves?

Are we not recognizing the sweetness of our life?

Is everything all work and no play?

Are our fears "eating away" at us?

Do we have trouble digesting our own goodness?

Music Therapies for Digestion

1. THERAPEUTIC MUSIC AND RHYTHM STYLES

Peristalsis is the body's rate or rhythm of digestion. It resonates with tones and rhythms, and these can be strengthened. Because of this, the digestive system is one of the easiest systems to influence with music, particularly with tones and rhythms.

Chamber music, pastorales, waltzes, and music from the Romantic period are particularly beneficial. The Romantic period lasted from the late 1700s to the early 1900s and included composers such as Liszt, Schubert, Brahms, Mussorgsky and Strauss.

Chamber Music

Chamber music, written to be performed in a room of a private house or a small hall, became increasingly popular during the Romantic period. In chamber music, each performer has a part of his or her own to play.

Just from a symbolic aspect, we should be able to see the connection between how chamber music is performed and how the digestive system operates with its individual organs. Since the stomach is the primary storehouse of digestion, this organ can be more easily influenced by chamber music. It can be a wonderful form of music to bring the individual activities of the digestive organs of the body into harmony.

Pastorales and Waltzes

Within the Romantic period, two other forms of music seem to stand out—at least for their therapeutic aspects. These are the pastorale and the waltz. The pastorale was a gentle piece of music that suggested the calmness and peace of the countryside. Its softness eases tension and calms the mental stresses creating indigestion and other digestive imbalances.

The waltz, a dance step in a triple meter, also achieved its strongest popularity during the Romantic period and came to epitomize the Romantic spirit of the time.

Although the waltz dominated the attention of many composers, Johann Strauss is still considered its king. His rhythms and melodies are soothing and uplifting and have great therapeutic value for the digestive system. I frequently recommend Strauss waltzes to those who overindulge in their eating upon occasion, such as Thanksgiving and other holidays meals.

MUSIC FOR THE DIGESTIVE SYSTEM

Composer	Work	Effect
Beethoven	Symphony no. 6 in F Major (Pastorale)	beneficial to all digestive aspects; most effective when played during the meal to make eating more enjoyable and with less side effects
Mozart	Symphony no. 9 in E Flat Major	beneficial at meal times to facilitate digestion and prevent indigestion
Strauss	Tales from the Vienna Woods On the Beautiful, Blue Danube all Strauss waltzes	beneficial to all digestive imbalances, particularly effective for indigestion and discomfort from overeating
Brahms	Liebslieder Waltzes	good for indigestion and general eating discomforts

2. TONAL AND INSTRUMENTAL THERAPIES

In Eastern traditions, the chakra or level of consciousness that is associated with and directs the digestive system is the solar plexus chakra. The solar plexus chakra is linked to the level of the subconscious mind that controls general digestive activities and the organs of digestion.

The solar plexus chakra influences the adrenals and helps the body assimilate nutrients. This chakra is the center that is beneficial to focus upon for all digestive imbalances, most intestinal problems, and even some psychosomatic illnesses. As with all centers and levels of consciousness, specific tones and musical keys, along with specific instruments, are more likely to impact upon the digestive system.

A Natural Third

The third or third note above the key note of the musical scale we are using is most beneficial for digestion. If we are using a generic scale of middle C, this would be music in the key of E or E flat. A natural third in music is simple and uncluttered. It is used in music to create a sense of comfort, and thus can be grounding and stimulating to digestion. When overstuffed, the third can even stimulate movement.

If we are using the scale for our own astrological sign (more personal for us), then we would use the third tone of that scale. For example, if we are a Virgo, then we might use the scale of F. The third tone of the musical scale in F is A. This means that music in the key of A might be used to balance a Virgo's digestive system (see Appendix B for more information).

Flutes and Other Woodwind Instruments

Regardless of the individual tone or key, flutes and other woodwind instruments are the most beneficial instruments for the digestive system. The flute, one of the oldest instruments in the world, is considered in many traditions to be an extension of the body because it is played through breath.

Breath is one of the two primary requirements for life, the other being food. Woodwind instruments were considered a link to nature. From a symbolic aspect, they are a link to balancing our own nature, especially through digestion.

Music to Stimulate the Solar Plexus Chakra

To aid in balancing and healing digestive system imbalance, you can play the musical selections found on the opposite page. They will help to stimulate the solar plexus chakra or level of the subconscious corresponding to the digestive system.

Remember to visualize the music surrounding you and then flowing into you through the solar plexus chakra. See and feel it filling you and balancing the digestive system.

 MUSIC FOR THE SOLAR PLEXUS CHAKRA

Type	Composer	Work
key of E and E flat, both major and minor	Mozart	The Magic Flute
	Carlos Nakai	all works
all chamber music	Brahms	Symphony no. 4 in E Minor
all waltzes and pastorales	Beethoven	Moonlight Sonata (Sonata no. 14), Opus 27, no. 2
	Bach	Suite in B Minor for the Flute and Strings
	Debussy	Afternoon of a Faun, Syrinx

3. VOCAL REMEDIES FOR DIGESTION

 We can use vocal tones and remedies in various forms to interact with the digestive system. In Chapter 2, the process for using the toning, chanting, and affirming methods in healing were discussed. If you're not familiar with those methods, it might be beneficial to go back and review that discussion.

Toning

 The table at the bottom of the page shows the vowel sounds and mantram most beneficial for the digestive system.

To enhance the effects of these sounds, we can tone them in the appropriate musical key. If you are using your own personal musical scale, use its third interval. If you do not know or are unsure of the scale, use middle C. In this case, the pitch will be E (or E flat). Again, an inexpensive pitch pipe will help you with this.

Chakra	Vowel Sound	Mantra
SOLAR PLEXUS	short o (*aw*)	ram (*rahm*)

You may also prefer to perform the toning while playing one of the pieces of music suggested earlier. Simply play the music in the background and softly tone the vowel sound or the mantram. Allow it to find its own rhythm.

Performing the toning or chanting to the flute music of Carlos Nakai or a Strauss waltz is not only beneficial for the digestive system, but also most enjoyable to our spirit as well.

Affirming

We can also use many wonderful affirmations and words of power to benefit the digestive system. These are particularly beneficial if we can determine some of the metaphysical or hidden issues affecting the condition. Use these as a starting point to creating your own affirmations.

As you create your personal affirmations, keep in mind the role and function of the digestive system. It has to do with taking in and assimilating nutrients.

I am nourished by all of life!
I benefit from all within my life!
I experience only what I need and can find joy in!
I release all that is not beneficial to me!
I am at peace with who I am!
I taste the sweetness of life!

I am nourishing to myself and others!
I am filled with joy and blessings!

WORDS OF POWER

Jehoval Aloah
Va Daath
yah-hoh-vah-ay-
loh-ah-vuh-dawth

"The Divine Made Manifest in
the Heart of the Mind"

This is the Hebrew name for that aspect
of the Divine that serves to manifest all
things in life. The mind is at the heart of
all that manifests, and thus this is a name
that can be chanted or toned to counter
the effects that negative thinking has
upon our overall health.

Raphael
rah-fah-ehl

"Angel of Beauty, Brightness,
and Healing"

Michael
mee-kah-ehl

"Angel of Protection and Balance"

4. MUSIC AND MOVEMENT THERAPIES

 In conjunction with the therapeutic music, several kinds of movements are beneficial to the digestive system. In particular, waltzes and stretching exercises can assist us in working with indigestion or digestive system imbalances.

Waltzing

I recommend that everyone learn some version of a waltz step. We do not have to perform a waltz, but by moving with the waltz rhythms, we facilitate digestion. Dancing a waltz is also a great boost to the spirit. Sometimes waltzing can help to ease or lift our depression, making digestion much easier on the body.

Five to ten minutes of easy waltzing (and yes, you can waltz by yourself!) before and after eating can be wonderful to your overall energy. Remember to see waltzing and the stretching exercises as a process for combining music and dance therapy.

Do not worry if your movements aren't smooth or exactly as depicted. Do not force the movements, and if painful or uncomfortable, stop! Do the best you can, and remember whatever you can do will enhance the beneficial impact upon the digestive system's imbalance.

Waltzing and the following exercises are simple movements that can be used to aid the digestive system. Perform the movements as a series. Take your time with them. Feel free to improvise within them in conjunction to the music you employ.

Some good pieces of music to play while waltzing or doing the stretching exercise include any Strauss waltzes, Debussy's *Afternoon of a Faun* or his *Syrinx,* and Tchaikovsky's *Symphony no. 5 in E Minor.*

Stretching Exercises

There are also stretching and slow, yoga-like movements that are beneficial to perform both before and after eating. When used with the right music, these movements facilitate digestion and help prevent problems and discomforts. Any kind of movement or exercise a half hour prior to eating will also diminish the appetite.

Together these positions relax the internal organs of digestion, releasing tension—particularly that held in the stomach area and small intestine. It is stretching and relaxing to the entire alimentary canal and the internal organs of digestion.

Figure A

1. The first series of movements is done from a curled position to one of openness. Begin by taking a kneeling position (Figure A).

Figure B

2. Then lower the buttocks to rest on the heels and then slowly stretch the body forward, tucking the head to the knees (Figure B).

   Stretch the arms forward and then back, bringing them to the sides.

   From this position begin slow rhythmic breathing. As you inhale, arch and curl your back up keeping your head to the knees. At its farthest stretch, hold. As you exhale allow the back to uncurl, relaxing. Repeat five times.

3. Slowly straighten the trunk while still kneeling with the buttocks upon the heels.

   Using your arms as a brace against the floor, bring your hips up and forward, slowly arching back as far as is comfortable (Figure C).

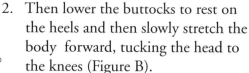

Figure C

Perform this as you inhale. Allow yourself to feel the stretch. As you hold this position for a count of four, also hold your breath. As you exhale, allow your back to straighten and your buttocks and hips to return to rest. Repeat this five more times.

Figure D

4. From these, you can then move to a fourth movement which may be a little more difficult. It is taken directly from yoga. It is the *asana* known as the bow pose (Figure D).

Begin by lying flat, face down. Bend the legs over the thighs, and arch the back at the same time. If possible, reach back with your hands and grab your ankles. Pull the head, chest and thighs up as high as is comfortable.

Once you become comfortable with this posture, begin slow rocking forward and back. This exercise creates a powerful massage for all of the abdominal organs, especially those associated with digestion.

Ted Andrews

NOTES

MUSIC THERAPY FOR NON-MUSICIANS

SUMMARY OF MUSICAL GUIDELINES FOR DIGESTION

Solar Plexus Chakra

TONE	E and E flat
VOWEL	short o (*aw*)
MANTRAM	ram
INSTRUMENT	flute, woodwinds
STYLE	waltz, romance

Complimentary

IMBALANCE	INSTRUMENT	KEY
abdominal cramps	flutes, woodwinds	E
belching	flutes	E
diabetes (pancreas)	strings, oboe, cello	D, B
heartburn	orchestra	E, F
indigestion	flutes, waltzes	D, E
liver problems	strings	D
nausea	Native American flutes	E, G
stomach discomfort (general)	waltz rhythms, chamber music	E, E flat
ulcers	flute, woodwinds	D, E

Digestion Therapies

SOUNDS	COLORS	AROMAS
(*aw, ah*)	yellow	mints
(*oh, ah*)	yellow, citrine	peppermint, lemon
(*oh, ee*)	violet	bay, eucalyptus
(*ah, ay*)	indigo	lemon, spearmint
(*oh, ah*)	pale yellow	peppermint
(*oh*)	lemon yellow	pine, juniper berry
(*ah, eh*)	ice blue	peppermint, nutmeg, wisteria
—	pale yellow	mints
(*oh, ah*)	blue and yellow combinations	nutmeg, peppermint

*In accordance with the Laws of Nutritional
transmutation, the emotions we feel,
the thoughts we think, even the words we speak,
all create certain chemicals and chemical reactions
within our bodies...that affect every single cell,
tissue and organ of our bodies.*[1]

---

[1] Bob L. Owen, *You Don't Have to Die Sick* (Cannon Beach, Oregon: Health Hope Publishing House, 1994), p. 7.

Chapter 5

Music Therapies for Elimination

Eimination is the body's process for filtering and excretion Most people assume the eliminative process involves only the bowels, urinary tract and related organs. However, we also eliminate wastes through the lungs and through the skin. For our purposes, this chapter will focus upon the organs of the bladder, bowels, kidneys, and urinary tract.

Our Elimination System

The *kidneys*, with two primary functions, are critical to the eliminative process. First, they serve to filter the blood plasma into separate substances: those substances the body needs and those it does not. Secondly, the kidneys aid in the excretion of unneeded substances.

Small tubes called *ureters* connect the kidneys to the urinary bladder and these tubes transport the urine from the kidneys to the *urinary bladder*. The urinary bladder empties its contents through a tube called a *urethra* leading to an external opening through which we urinate.

Ted Andrews   111

The small intestine ends where it joins the *colon* or large intestine. The small intestine's primary function is to absorb water and eliminate digestion residue. The colon itself ends in the muscular region of the *rectum*. The sphincter muscle in the rectum retains feces or wastes until it can be discharged through the *anus*. When the small intestine and colon are grouped together, they are generally referred to as the *bowels*.

Problems With Elimination

Any problem with any aspect of elimination should cause us to examine issues of letting go and holding on within our lives. Elimination problems can result in bladder infections, blocked bowels, constipation, diarrhea, and kidney aliments.

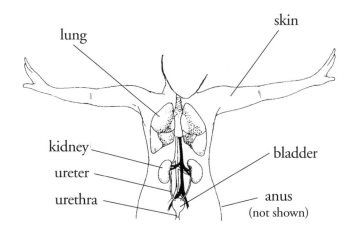

Problems with the kidneys, for example, can be agitated by emotions and mental attitudes that reflect their function. Kidneys serve to filter, so lack of discernment and discrimination in our life can put stress upon their functioning. Exposing ourselves to unwarranted criticism from ourselves or others will also stress the kidneys.

Problems with the urinary bladder or any aspect of its tract can be aggravated by anxiety and anger. Ask yourself whether you are "pissed off" at someone or something. Being forced to let go of things in our life that we find beneficial can also irritate urinary conditions. Incontinence occurs frequently in the elderly, often showing up when a job or loved one has been lost. Incontinence can be symbolic of a plug being pulled on an aspect of our lives or feeling as if control in life has been lost.

The bowels are symbols of release and letting go. Pain or problems in any area of the bowels (small intestine and colon) may reflect issues related to releasing something or someone in our life which no longer benefits us.

A variety of emotions can cause or worsen eliminative problems:

- frustration,
- anxiety,

- fear of letting go,
- anger,
- sense of uselessness or hopelessness,
- selfishness,
- lack of control,
- feeling unneeded,
- needing approval, and
- lack of support.

If eliminative problems start to surface, they offer us an opportunity to focus on and clarify issues in our lives. With a little self-examination, we may be able to discern the some of the factors contributing to the imbalance.

When eliminative problems arise, we might ask ourselves the following questions:

Do we feel we have no control in our life?

Are we feeling useless or in the way?

Are we afraid of letting go?

Are we hanging onto the past even though it is not to our benefit?

Are we not eliminating who or what is no longer beneficial within our life?

Are we not discerning the good from the bad?

Are we being too critical of ourselves?

Are we not releasing and learning from our failures or mistakes?

Are we hanging on to childhood fears?

Do we feel as if life is passing us by?

Do we have a "better the devil we know than the one we don't" kind of attitude?

Music Therapies for Elimination

1. THERAPEUTIC MUSIC AND RHYTHM STYLES

There is a strong correlation between the music and rhythm styles affecting digestion and those affecting elimination. The two systems are so closely linked that there can be overlap. If we ease the digestive processes, we also then help ease the eliminative phase. For example, waltz rhythms and music will relieve discomfort when we have overeaten. This occurs in part because the eliminative process is strengthened as well.

On the other hand, there are music rhythms and styles that are very compatible with elimination itself, both physiologically as well as symbolically. Two of these in particular—blues and spirituals—are often considered America's greatest contribution to the music of the world.

Blues

Blues is a strand of jazz more generally slow moving and sensuous. Jazz is described in later chapters. Blues tunes are slow songs woven with jazz music and rhythms, typically sung or played to release and reflect sadness.

No one knows exactly where or when the blues were born, but the form originated in the South among the Blacks. Over the years, the blues has developed into a powerful form of musical expression.

Blues singers and performers do not always stick to perfect pitch, preferring instead to use wavering tones according to their feelings. From a symbolic aspect, their actions reflect a need for each of us to find our own expression and rhythm in spite of the past.

Blues can help us let go of the past, recognizing it for its influence upon us while moving into our own direction. In essence, we have a responsibility to find our own physiological rhythms and work with them.

Spirituals

Spirituals are another kind of music beneficial to the eliminative system. A spiritual is a revival type of hymn, strongly rhythmic and based upon folk tunes from the British Isles and Africa. Spirituals grew out of despair, depression, and hopelessness and are performed to release the despair and to awaken hope. From just its symbolic aspect, we should be able to

see the possible connection of using spirituals to aid the eliminative system.

Selected Music to Aid in Elimination

The following, more classical style blues works are beneficial for the eliminative system. These can aid in the strengthening, balancing, and healing of the urinary system.

MUSIC FOR THE ELIMINATION SYSTEM

Composer	Work	Effect
Ravel	Sonata for Violin and Piano	strengthens and stimulates the eliminative process
Milhaud	Le Creation du Monde	benefits indigestion and balances both constipation and diarrhea
Copland	Four Piano Blues Piano Fantasy	strengthens and heals the eliminative process

In addition, there are a great number of blues and spiritual singers whose music can be beneficial. The following list is but a sampling and should be consider merely a starting point:

- Billie Holiday,
- Louis Armstrong and Bessie Smith,
- Ray Charles,
- Mahalia Jackson, and
- Pete Seeger.

These singers and their performances provide a wonderful tonic for both body and spirit.

Their music can be used to create homeostasis or regularity for the eliminative system and to stimulate greater awareness of the hidden issues behind the imbalance. I highly recommend them for anyone who truly wishes to experience the emotional power of music more personally.

2. Tonal And Instrumental Therapies

As with all the major systems of the body, the elimination system also responds more strongly to instruments, key notes, and music that stimulates the spleen chakra.

Brass and Percussion Instruments

Traditionally, brass instruments are used for blues and spirituals. Although the piano is frequently used in both, brass instruments are much more effective. A blues trumpet, saxophone, or trombone can have a great impact.

Made of brass tubing, these instruments are played by blowing air through compressed lips and range in size and shape from the trumpet to the tuba. The trumpet and trombone have been particularly important to the development of jazz, blues, and big band sounds.

Music: Keys of D, E Minor, and Minor Thirds

In musical composition, minor tones are used as a way of earthing energies. They bring the experience to an individual level in which the individual can respond more easily. By using the keys of D and

E minor, we can stimulate the feelings and draw greater sympathy from the listener.

In blues singing, there is often a simultaneous sounding of the minor thirds of chords. Minor thirds are intervals of sadness, touching emotional responses. In music, a minor third can hint of a lack of direction or of a foreshadowing. The expression of the music in turn creates a response in the body: where there was no movement, it now begins.

Music to Stimulate the Spleen Chakra

In the Eastern tradition, the chakra that most strongly impacts the eliminative system is the second center or spleen chakra. The term spleen chakra is the name for a level of the subconscious mind that controls and directs the activities of elimination. Stimulating the spleen chakra through specific tones and instruments can balance and heal the organs of elimination.

The musical selections in the table on the following page are beneficial for stimulating the spleen chakra and for balancing and healing the eliminative system and its organs.

MUSIC FOR THE SPLEEN CHAKRA

Type	Composer	Work
key of D and E minor	Ravel	Sonata for Violin and Piano
minor thirds		
	Bach	Toccata and Fugue in D Minor
	Maynard Ferguson	any music
	Copland	Quiet City
	Stravinsky	Rite of Spring
	Louis Armstorng, Miles Davis, Dizzie Gilespie	trumpet music
	Coleman Hawkins, John Coltrane, Charlie Parker	saxophone music
	Billie Holiday	all music
	B.B. King	all music

3. Vocal Remedies for Elimination

 We can tone and chant to create vocal sounds to interact with the eliminative system. For those who may have an inclination to sing, toning in a blues style can be most beneficial and quite enjoyable.

Toning

 The vowel sound and mantram in the table below are beneficial for the eliminative system.

To enhance the effects of these sounds, tone them in an appropriate musical key. If using the generic, middle C scale, tone the sounds in D or E minor. If using a more personal musical scale, use that scale's second or minor third. Refer to Appendix B for additional information on creating a more personal musical scale.

You may also wish to perform the toning and chanting while listening to one of the pieces of music suggested earlier. Play the music in the background

Chakra	Vowel Sound	Mantra
SPLEEN	long o (*oh*)	vam

and softly tone the vowel sound or mantram. Allow it to find its own length and rhythm.

If you have a favorite blues piece, singing the mantram or the vowel sound along with that music can have a dynamic effect upon your system. Remember to visualize the system balancing and healing as you do this.

Affirming

Dynamic affirmations and words of power can be used to benefit the eliminative system. One of the most effective ways of influencing the elimination system through affirmations is to create your own blues song incorporating an affirmation. Keep it simple, but remember the more creative you are with this, the greater the effect. Even what seems to be a silly "blues affirmations" can be a healing tool.

Try to make your affirmation a two-line song. The first line states the problem and the second line states the affirmation that heals. The following may seem silly, but laughter is also healing. Anytime we become creative, it heals us.

For constipation, try listening to some B. B. King and then sing the following two-line song:

My BOWELS won't move.
(ba-BAH-ba-ba)
But NOW they do.
(ba-BAH-ba-ba)

The following sample affirmations can be used to benefit the eliminative system. They can be even more beneficial if we can determine the metaphysical or hidden issues affecting the condition. Use them as a starting point for creating your own affirmations.

As you create your personal affirmations, keep in mind the role and function of the eliminative system: the filtering and eliminating of waste.

I am free of the past!
I embrace life!
I hold onto that which nourishes me!
I am of benefit to myself and others!
I release all that is not good in my life!
My fears are unfounded!
I release what is no longer beneficial to me.
I am free of the past!
I am useful and beneficial to myself and others!

Ted Andrews

WORDS OF POWER

Shaddai El Chai
shah-dye-ehl-kye

"The Almighty Living God"

This is the aspect of the Divine that reveals the foundation of our lives. It opens us to revelations of what is beneficial to us and what is not, strengthening those aspects of our life which can bless.

Gabriel
gah-bree-ehl

"Angel of Hope, Illumination, and Love"

4. MUSIC AND MOVEMENT THERAPIES

We can use several movements to strengthen the eliminative system. Perform them only to the degree you are comfortable with them, and don't be afraid to adapt them.

If you happen to have a weak eliminative system, these combinations of yoga asanas and free movements can be of benefit. However, consult your physician and discuss the use of these movements before undertaking them.

The following movements are soothing, relaxing, and easily performed. Their effectiveness can be increased by performing them against soft but easily heard background of music.

The following musical pieces are beneficial when performing these movements:

- music of Billie Holiday,
- music of B.B. King,
- Copland's *Piano Fantasy*, and
- old time spirituals.

Movement for Elimination

As with all of the exercises in this book, five to ten minutes is all that is necessary to gain some benefit from them. Begin slowly and easily, only performing the movements to your level of comfort. Some is better than none at all, but don't force the movements. With every movement, know that your system is strengthened and the imbalance is healed. All energy follows thought, but when the thought is combined with the right music and movement, the effects are tremendously amplified!

The first set of movements stretches and flexes the inner organs of both digestion and elimination. They also help strengthen the muscles controlling the bladder.

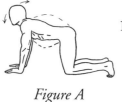

Figure A

1. Begin on all fours like a cat. As you inhale, raise the head up and lower the spine, bending it as if to touch the floor with your stomach (Figure A).

2. Feel the stretch and hold your breath.

3. As you exhale, lower the head and raise the spine, arching it upwards. Clench and hold the buttock muscles for a count of four, and then return to the beginning position.

4. Repeat this five to ten times, keeping the movements slow and controlled.

The second exercise, a Pelvic Circle, eases the pain and discomfort of elimination when constipated.

Figure B

1. Begin by standing, feet shoulder's length apart, arms at side, relaxed. Bend both knees slightly. Slowly begin to circle your pelvis in one direction (Figure A).

The circling should be slow and as smooth as possible in the beginning. Try to keep your ribs and trunk still so that only the lower part of your body is moving.

Figure C

2. As you get more into the movement and the rhythm of the music, adjust your speed to be slower and faster. Then perform the circles in the opposite direction (Figure C).

There is a lot of room for improvising here, particularly with the music you will be using. Improvising is fine, but

*be sure to complete circles in
both directions.*

*As you get into it, see the move-
ments as stabilizing, strengthening and healing your eliminative
system.*

NOTES

MUSIC THERAPY FOR NON-MUSICIANS

Summary of Musical Guidelines
for Elimination

Chakra	Spleen	Base
TONE	D, D sharp (*re*)	C (*do*)
VOWEL	long o (*oh*)	long u (*oo*)
MANTRAM	vam	lam
INSTRUMENT	percussion, brass tones, brass	percussion
STYLE	rhapsodies, blues, African, Hispanic	African, reggae

Complimentary

IMBALANCE	INSTRUMENT	KEY
bladder	strings	E, E flat, B
bowels	blues instruments	D minor
constipation	flute, strings, spiritual rhythms	E
diarrhea	blues horns (trombone, trumpet)	E flat
kidneys	brass	D, E

Elimination Therapies

SOUNDS	COLORS	AROMAS
—	indigo and orange combinations	lilac
(*oh*)	orange, orange-yellow	juniper berry
(*aw*)	yellow	rosemary, peppermint, lemon
(*aw*)	blue and orange combinations	nutmeg
(*oh, aw*)	yellow, orange	lemon

Life is given to us for the perfection of our nature and thus the betterment of mankind. The betterment of our nature cannot occur without honest labor.[1]

---

[1]Hanna Kroeger, *New Dimensions in Healing Yourself* (Boulder, Colorado: Chapel of Miracles, 1991), p. 91.

Chapter 6

Music Therapies for the Glands

All things have a purpose, but we need to look for those functions and apply some understanding. Although we treat each system individually, they all influence each other and none is any more important than the others. They all have their work.

We must each find the methods which work most effectively for our individual systems. That's why the therapies provided in this book are meant to be used only as guidelines.

The Glandular System

The glandular (endocrine) system is complicated. It overlaps the activities of other systems and shares their organs. Because of this, the information presented here is general, but will provide a starting point for your own understanding of the glandular system. As you explore the imbalances associated with this system, you will probably need to seek out additional information for your individual situation.

The endrocrine system involves all of the glandular activities of the body and has an intimate relationship with the nervous system. One of the functions of the glandular system is to regulate and direct the functions of the various bodily organs. The *hormones,* or chemicals secreted by the glands, excite or inhibit organ activity.

The glandular system greatly influences the overall body's immunity, although there is still a great deal to understand about how this works.

Many of the glands making up the glandular system are treated in association with other bodily

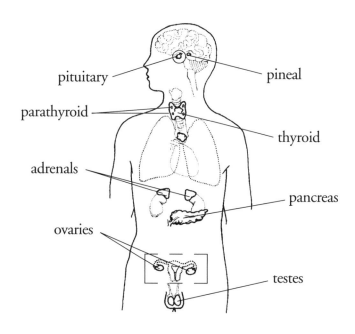

systems. For example, the mammary glands, gonads, and ovaries are often treated as part of the reproductive system. For the purposes of this text, we will do likewise. In addition, some organs, such as the liver, have glandular activities, so the glandular system is one of the most difficult to work with and describe.

There are many glands in the body, as well as organs that have glandular, hormone-secreting activities. For our purposes, we will focus upon five glands: the pituitary, the thyroid, the adrenals, the thymus, and the pineal.

The Pituitary

The *pituitary* is like the overseer or governor of all glandular activity within the body, influencing the activities of most of the major glands. The pituitary is very critical to the entire immune system of the body.

Pituitary problems are usually centered in how we are governing our life or how we are allowing others to influence it.

The Thyroid

The *thyroid* serves as the thermostat for the body, regulating the overall body metabolism. Metabolism is the sum of all the body processes involved in building up and breaking down of tissue.

> Every cell within the body is a little power plant. Each cell oxidizes food and sets energy free. This energy powers all life activity....When the doctor speaks of your metabolism, he is referring to the speed of the fires in these tiny power plants.[2]

The thyroid's activity determines whether or not we have a sluggish metabolism or a rapid one.

Thyroid problems can reflect issues associated with expression and how much or how little we may feel we are accomplishing or expressing within our life.

The Adrenals

The *adrenals* serve several functions. They assist in the breakdown of proteins, and they stimulate the metabolism in times of need or emergency. They are our fight (protection) or flight (self-preservation) glands. Problems with them can be aggravated through anxiety and worries over issues within our life.

The Thymus

The *thymus*, like the pituitary, has a great influence on body immunity. It is critical to the development of our early immune system in childhood. Although often believed to naturally atrophy as puberty approaches, new studies in this gland's activ-

---

[2] James H. Otto, Cloyd Julian, and J. Edward Thether, *Modern Health* (New York: Holt, Rhinehart and Winston, Inc., 1971), pp. 287-288.

ity level and function indicate this is not necessarily the case.

Currently, researchers are examining whether in adults the thymus can be stimulated again into activity. With the rise of new bacteria and diseases, many people believe this is key to strengthening and developing increased immunity.

Thymus problems may reflect issues associated with infectious thoughts and attitudes of others and ourselves.

The Pineal

The *pineal* is directly linked to the nervous system and to the sexual functions of growth. Like the thymus, the pineal gland seems to reach its greatest size in childhood; thus it, too, links to the early development of immunity and perceptions.

In the East, it has long been a symbol of higher perceptions—both psychically and spiritually.

Problems with the Glands

There are a variety of emotions and mental attitudes that can increase glandular imbalances. The following are the more common ones:

- fears (general),
- worries,

- doubts,
- impatience,
- procrastination,
- lack of sympathy,
- lack of vision and insight,
- fear of failure,
- fear of the past,
- lack of honor,
- anxiety, and
- lack of responsibility.

Asking some basic questions will provide insight into the what issues might be upsetting this particular imbalance:

Do we feel in control of our lives?

Are we allowing others to control our lives?

Are we not claiming our power or doing it inappropriately?

Are we not responding to issues within our life?

Are others not responding to us?

Are we allowing the attitudes of others to affect us?

Are we expressing ourselves appropriately?

Have we forgotten to enjoy the sweetness of life?

Are we feeling depressed lately?

Music Therapies for the Glands

1. THERAPEUTIC MUSIC AND RHYTHM STYLES

A variety of musical styles benefit the glandular system. The most beneficial are symphonies, sonatas, organ music, drones, and nocturnes.

Symphonies and Sonatas

A symphony is an orchestral work, usually consisting of three or four movements. A sonata, one of the earliest forms for a small group of instrumentalists, is a version of the symphony that is very effective for the endocrine system.

Symphonic music is good for both the endocrine and the nervous systems, harmonizing the glandular activity of the nervous system and organs of the body. In Chapter 8, we will examine additional effects of symphonies on the nervous system.

Organ Music, Droning, and Nocturnes

Organ music can be a powerful tonic for the glandular system. The organ, one of the oldest instruments, dates back almost 2000 years. Technically a wind instrument with pipes, it has great power. The organ can create a droning effect which can act strongly upon the body. Other powerful droning instruments for healing are bagpipes and digeridoos.

Nocturnes are night songs. They have a calming nature with long melodic lines and can help with hyperactivity and insomnia. They can be played during sleep to strengthen and balance the glandular system.

Selected Music to Aid the Glandular System

The table on the following page lists pieces of music which are beneficial for the glandular system, strengthening, balancing, and helping to heal it.

Music for the Glands

Composer	Work	Effect
Handel	Water Music	a good tonic for the entire system
Chopin	Nocturne	soothes and strengthens the whole system; a good tonic for the immune system
	Etudes	helps establish harmony among the glands and the nervous system
Beethoven	Symphony no. 3 (Eroica)	wonderful for the adrenal glands, especially if overtaxed
	Symphony no. 7	strengthens the pituitary and thus all of the glands, improving immunity
Mendelssohn	Scottish Symphony	balances thyroid and strengthens personal expression
Tchaikovsky	Capriccio Italien	heals entire system; beneficial to reproduction and immunity

2. TONAL AND INSTRUMENTAL THERAPIES

Music stimulating to the brow chakra can influence the glandular system. This system responds strongly to string instruments, crystal bowls, and organ music, as well as music in the key of A or A flat.

The Brow Chakra

The brow chakra is most strongly associated with the glandular system, although the crown also has a great influence. The brow chakra is the level of the subconscious mind that directs and influences the major glands of the body. It also affects the synapses of the brain and it has links to the eyes, sinuses, and facial aspects of the body.

In traditional metaphysics, the brow chakra is also the center for higher perceptions and clairvoyance and also the seat of the feminine and magnetic aspects of the body.

String Instruments, Crystal Bowls, and Organ Music

The brow chakra and the glandular system respond strongly to string instruments, particularly violins and cellos, and all droning instruments. Drones are usually pipes or strings that can play one or sometimes a few tones, setting up a strong vibration, such as the bagpipes or the digeridoo. Many folk traditions have some kind of droning instrument.

Tibetan singing bowls and crystal bowls can also be used to effect the brow chakra and glandular system. Crystal bowls are powerful modern droning instruments that have dynamic healing capabilities.[3]

The organ creates a powerful droning effect, but has much greater versatility. Bach's *Toccata and Fugue in D Minor* is a powerful organ piece which stimulates not only the adrenal glands but also other organs and systems, including the muscular system.

Music in the Key or A or A Flat and the Sixth Interval

We can also use music in the key of A or A flat, both major or minor, to act upon the glandular system. If you are using a more personal musical scale, use the sixth interval of music written in the key of that scale. The sixth interval stimulates a sense of well-being with more to come and awakens a sense of nourishment.

For more information on a personal music scale, refer to Appendix B.

---

[3] For more information on crystal bowls, refer to my book listed in the bibliography.

Music to Stimulate the Brow Chakra

The following musical selections are beneficial to stimulating the brow chakra and to aid in balancing and strengthening the glandular system.

Remember to visualize the music surrounding you and then flowing into you through the chakra center. See and feel it filling you and balancing the corresponding system.

 MUSIC FOR THE BROW CHAKRA

Type	Composer	Work
key of A and A flat, both major and minor	Berlioz	Symphonie Fantastique
	Mendelssohn	String Quartet in A
all bagpipe music		
primitive and traditional folk instruments (droning)	Wagner	Evening Star from Tannhouser
	Franck	Nocturne, Symphony in D Minor
	Brahams	Lullaby
	Mozart	Symphony no. 29 in A Major

3. Vocal Remedies for the Glandular system

 We can use vocal remedies in various forms to interact with the glandular system: chants, mantras, words of power, singing, and toning.

Toning

 The vowel sound and mantra in the table below is most beneficial for the endocrine system.

To enhance the effects, tone them in their appropriate musical key. If using the generic scale of Middle C, then tone the vowel sound or mantram at the pitch of A. If using your own personal scale, then use the pitch provided for the brow chakra of your astrological sign.

To further enhance these efforts, you might also want to perform the toning while playing one of the musical pieces listed on the previous page. Play the music softly in the background for ten minutes as you perform the toning. Toning while playing Handel's *Water Music* is particularly useful.

Chakra	Vowel Sound	Mantra
BROW	long e (*ee*)	aum, om

Allow the toning to find its own rhythm. Remember to visualize the glands strengthening and balancing.

Affirming

Many wonderful affirmations and words of power can benefit the glandular system as well. Their energy is especially effective when we determine the hidden issue which may be causing our condition. Use these affirmations as a starting point for creating your own.

As you create your personal affirmations, keep in mind the role of the glandular system: to control and direct the glands. When creating your own affirmations, think about the role of the various glands which may be out of balance.

The following affirmations are effective in assisting the endocrine system:

I am in control of my life and all I experience!

I respond to life with joy and ability!

I am immune to all of life's troubles.

I embrace the sweetness and joy in life.

I am powerful and effective in life!

I express myself with joy and ease!

I am powerful and free!

I am free to enjoy and participate in life!

Words of Power

Jehovah Elohim
yah-hoh-veh-eh-loh-heem

"The Divine Perfection through Creation"

This is that aspect of the Divine that manifests through creation and through understanding. It is that aspect of the Divine which helps us to understand our own perfection.

Eheieh
eh-huh-yeh

"I am that I am"

This is the name for that aspect of the Divine within us that already knows that we are perfection. We are the Divine in the making. It reminds us that the Divine is an everpresent fact in our life.

Tzaphkiel
zahf-keye-ehl

"Angel of Comfort and Understanding"

4. MUSIC AND MOVEMENT THERAPIES

Movement and dance can also be used with music to stimulate and strengthen the glandular system. If the gland that is imbalanced is associated more specifically with another system of the body, perform those movements first. Then perform the following movements to reinforce their overall strength.

The following movement is a variation of the yoga asana know as the cobra. It is stretching and strengthening to the entire gland and lymph system, helping to bring all of the glands into harmony with each other.

Begin by choosing a piece of music appropriate for the endocrine system. This exercise is enhanced by visualizing ourselves as a snake with all of its symbolic significance. The snake has been a symbol of healing in many societies because of its ability to shed its skin—a symbolic death and rebirth. Visualizing this kind of transformation is strengthening to the entire glandular system, especially to glandular influence upon our immunity.

1. Lay flat upon the ground or floor for support

2. Stretch your arms out in front of you.

   Stretching helps release any tension you may be feeling. Relax as much as possible.

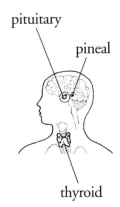

pituitary

pineal

thyroid

3. Breathe deeply and smoothly, allowing the music to surround you. Slowly bring your hands back in and rest under your chin.

4. Breathe deeply and slowly raise your head. Visualize your pineal and pituitary coming to life.

5. Stretch your neck up slowly and easily, as your thyroid is awakened and balanced.

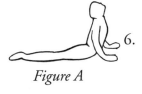

Figure A

6. Then slowly raise your shoulders, gradually pushing upward with your arms so the chest (thymus) and trunk (adrenals) of the body are raised up (Figure A).

The hips and legs remain flat on the floor, the feet pointed straight out behind you.

7. Straighten the arms and tilt the head back as far as is comfortable. Stretch the legs and feet back behind you at the same time. Hold this position for a count of four, and then slowly relax back down to the floor in reverse.

8. Inhale slowly and deeply as you rise up. Hold your breath when you reach the top, and then exhale slowly as you lower back down. Repeat five to ten times.

The slower you move, the better. Again, do not force the stretch.

Visualize as you do this. Feel the music filling you as you perform this exercise. This is not only a good over-all stretch but also a strengthener for the glands.

Take your time, enjoying the stretch and the music!

SUMMARY OF MUSICAL GUIDELINES
FOR GLANDS

Chakra	Brow	Crown	Throat
TONE	A (*la*)	B (*ti*)	G (*sol*)
VOWEL	long e (*ee*)	long e (*ee*)	short e (*eh*)
MANTRAM	aum	om	ham
INSTRU- MENT	strings, harps, cello, crystal bowls	harp, violin, Tibetan bells and bowls	acoustic guitar
STYLE	nocturne, symphony	organ, drones	sonata, nocturne

Complimentary

IMBALANCE	INSTRUMENT	KEY
adrenal	percussions, rattles	D
allergies	harp, violin	F, A
breasts	harp, cello, violin	F
hyperactivity	harp, acoustic guitar	F sharp, G
immunity	strings, violin	A, F
lymph	strings, cello	A
thyroid	harpsichord, strings	G, G sharp

Gland Therapies

Sounds	Colors	Aromas
(*oh*)	orange and blue combinations	patchouli
(*ay, ee*)	indigo and orange	gardenia, eucalyptus
(*ay*)	pink, rose	rose, patchouli, frangipani
(*ay*)	teal, blues, emerald	wisteria, eucalyptus
(*ay, ee*)	emerald, blues	rose, lilac, frankincense, sage
(*ee*)	indigo, violet	lavender, sage
—	sky blue, teals	wisteria, lavender

The human body is designed for movement.
Movement is as natural and as important to life
as breathing. Like breathing, it fills us with energy.
It enables us to transcend our usual perceptions
and consciousness. Movement balances,
heals, awakens and energizes.[1]

---

[1] Ted Andrews, *Magickal Dance* (St. Paul, Minnesota: Llewellyn Publications, 1993), p. 4.

Chapter 7

Music Therapies for the Muscles

Movement is natural to the universe. We can find movement in plants, animals, and throughout the natural world. Movement is a basic to all living things, and it is an essential aspect of human life.

Our Muscular System

In human life, the muscular system of the body makes movement possible. The skeletal muscles enable us to move through space; giving form to our bodies.

Internal muscles perform many of the body's internal processes. Cardiac muscles work heart. The smooth muscles of the blood vessel walls help move the blood throughout the body. Muscles also aid in respiration and digestion.

Problems with Our Muscles

With so many muscles in the body, it is not possible to try to describe the activities of each within the confines of this text. If you do have a muscle

problem, it might be beneficial to examine the system those troublesome muscles belong to and determine their function.

Leg muscles, for example, enable us to move and maintain physical balance. Problems with our leg muscles may reflect movement, or lack of it, in our lives, as well as how much balance we have within our lives.

We generally use our arm muscles to reach, grasp, and hold. Problems with these muscles may indicate there are issues about what we are or are not embracing and holding within our life.

Contemplating the specific muscle problems can help determine some of the major issues affecting or aggravating the condition.

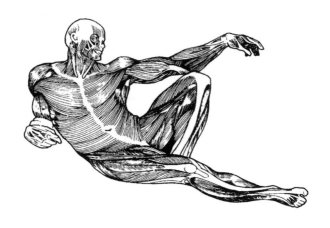

Is it is an ache?

A sprain?

A spasm?

A cramp?

Examining muscle problems can help us deal with the situation holistically. As you examine the muscular problem, ask the following questions. *Is it a chronic ache? What are we not dealing with regularly? Is it a reoccurring cramp? What are we trying to hold onto?*

Thinking about the kind of muscles causing problems can help determine the underlying issues that may have contributed to the imbalance. The following general emotions, when expressed by us or those close to us, can aggravate muscular discomfort, weaknesses, and imbalances:

- arrogance and conceit,
- mistrust,
- general worry and anxiety,
- blame,
- being overly critical,
- insecurity,
- fear of progress and growth,
- sadness, and
- depression.

If muscular problems arise, they can provide an opportunity to clarify important issues influencing us. With a little self-examination, we can obtain additional insight into those issues that might have caused the imbalance. With muscle problems, it is good to consider the following questions:

Are we overextending ourselves?

Are we overworked?

Are we not doing enough?

Are we allowing others to block us?

Are we resisting movement in our lives?

Are we afraid to grow?

Are we (or others around us) being too inflexible?

Are we stuck in outworn patterns?

Are we not taking time for relaxation and enjoyment?

Music Therapies for the Muscles

1. Therapeutic Music And Rhythm Styles

 For the most part, the muscles of the body respond to strong, clear percussion and bass rhythms. Keep in mind though that there will be some variations, depending upon the particular system the muscle belongs to. For example, the cardiac muscles respond strongly to Baroque rhythms, as we discussed in Chapter 3.

Hispanic, African, and Ethnic Rhythms

We can use Hispanic rhythms (salsa, etc.) to strengthen and loosen the muscles. African rhythms and marches can also be used to strengthen the muscles and the entire body. If you are of a particular ethnic group, look to the rhythmic styles of your heritage. These will more easily strengthen and heal muscles of your body.

Boogie-Woogie Style Rhythm

The popular boogie-woogie style, jazz with a driving, repetitive bass rhythm, is always good for a muscle "pick-me-up." Boogie-woogie music typically makes our muscles want to move—to dance.

Rap

Invariably, when speaking of rhythms at conferences and workshops, someone will ask me about the effects of good music versus bad—good rhythms versus bad rhythms. In the past few years, rap music has been brought up in these discussions.

Some individuals will even mention that they have heard rap music in some studies stifled or stopped the growth of plants. For the record, I have not come across any such study.

It is true that discordant music and rhythms can stimulate unpleasant emotions. In studies going back to the late 1930s, it was found that there is a direct link between music and rhythms and our emotional and physical health. Quite often people who ask such questions about good rhythms versus bad rhythms really don't understand the effects of rhythm.

Rap is one of the oldest forms of storytelling upon the planet, part of what I refer to as the bardic tradition in my earlier book *Sacred Sounds*. Not only was Rap used by the English bards, a rap method of storytelling was employed by the African griot, the Japanese zenza, the Norse skalds, the Navajo singers and many others.

The use of rhythms to tell poetic, mystical, and historic stories was common. The rhythms helped individuals to remember the stories, but also helped

to carry the story's message more strongly. The rhythms cause the words to have greater impact.

It is not the use of rhythms, but the words and the volume of the rhythms that determines the detrimental or beneficial effects.

Rhapsody and Overtures

Rhapsody, a free-form music style which arose in the nineteenth century, is beneficial to the muscular system. The composition was often heroic in feeling, with sweeping melodies and an improvised quality.

The overtures of many symphonies are also good for the muscles, providing a wonderful way to wake up the muscles. Overtures can be very powerful when performing stretching exercises and warm-ups.

Selected Music to Aid the Muscular System

The table on the following page lists beneficial music pieces for strengthening the muscular system and the overall body.

MUSIC FOR THE MUSCLE SYSTEM

Composer	Work	Effect
Mahler	Symphony no.1 in D Major	use for recovery from muscle injury; for background during physical therapy
Liszt[1]	Hungarian Rhapsodies	strengthens and rejuvenates muscles
Zolden	Peacock Variations, Variations on Hungarian folk songs	heals most major muscle groups; stimulates overall body energy
Gershwin	Rhapsody in Blue	stimulates insight into issues behind muscular imbalances
Wagner	Song of the Valkyries	use when muscles need a little stimulation
Elgar	Pomp and Circumstance	releases muscle tension due to sadness
Sousa	any of his marches	strengthens and uplifts muscles and the spirit

---

[1] Liszt did more with the rhapsody than any other composer, basing them on gypsy themes.

2. Tonal And Instrumental Therapies

We can use individual tones and instruments to stimulate the strengthening and balancing of muscles. The traditional chakra associated with the muscular system is the spleen, or second center. It is linked to the subconscious mind that controls the muscular system, part of the eliminative system, and even the reproductive system.

Music in the Key of D and D Minor

Certain tones, musical keys, and even instruments can be used to stimulate and balance the spleen chakra and corresponding biological responses. Music in the key of D major and D minor can be very beneficial—as well as all dance music.

Drums, Percussion Instruments, and Bass Tones

Drums (primitive or modern) and other percussion instruments can be used to stimulate and heal the muscles, along with repetitive rhythms of bass tones. Percussion rhythms are one of the most powerful means of impacting body muscles. Drums and percussion instruments can also stimulate and change metabolism, as well as induce altered states of

Ted Andrews   165

consciousness. These are among the most universal and oldest of all the healing instruments.

Music to Stimulate the Spleen Chakra

The musical selections in the following table stimulate the spleen chakra, strengthening the muscle responses within the body.

Remember to visualize the music surrounding you and then flowing into you through the spleen chakra. See and feel it filling you and balancing the muscular system.

 MUSIC FOR THE SPLEEN CHAKRA

Type	Composer	Work
key of D, major and minor	Pachelbel	Canon in D
all dance music; all drum music (primitive or modern)	Gluck	Dance of the Blessed Spirits
	Beethoven	La Sylphide
	Stravinsky	Fire Bird, Rite of Spring
	Liszt	Hungarian Rhapsodies

3. VOCAL REMEDIES FOR THE MUSCLES

We can use tones, chants, and affirmations in various forms to interact with the muscular system. See Chapter 2 for more information on toning, chanting, and affirming.

Toning

The vowel sound and mantram in the table below are the most beneficial for the muscular system.

To enhance the effects, tone the vowel sound or mantram in the appropriate musical key. If you are using the generic scale of middle C, use the pitch of D or D minor. If you are using a personal musical scale, use the second interval of that scale. Refer to Appendix B for additional information on how to create a personal musical scale.

You might also want to perform the toning while playing one of the suggested music pieces in the background. Simply play the music softly and slowly begin the toning process using the vowel, the

Chakra	Vowel Sound	Mantra
SPLEEN	long o (*oh*)	vahm

mantram, or both. Allow the toning to find its own rhythm.

Performing the toning to Stravinsky's *The Rite of Spring* is very healing to the muscles. Pachelbel's *Canon in D* also acts powerfully upon the muscles.

Affirming

Affirmations can also be used to benefit the muscular system. Again, they are particularly effective when we can determine the metaphysical effects or hidden issues behind the actual imbalance. If you are creating your own affirmations, keep in mind the role and function of the muscular system: to enable movement. Some beneficial affirmations for the muscles follow:

I am strong in all I do!

I move with ease and balance!

I achieve and grow daily!

I am strong and flexible!

I am relaxed and free!

I move into new realms with joy and strength!

I am free!

I move freely and with joy!

I am balanced as I move forward in life!

Chanting

There is a way of incorporating rhythm into the affirmations. It requires only a little more creativity, but the benefits are substantial. Instead of using a one line affirmation, use two lines. Both lines must rhyme and both lines must have the same number of syllables, as in the following example. In this way, they can be chanted in a rhythmic style that increases their power.

I am relaxed and free!

I am strong as a tree!

Keep the chants simple, but don't be afraid to experiment. You will surprise yourself how powerful something that may seem silly can be! Anytime we create, we activate healing energy!

Words of Power

Shaddai El Chai
shah-dye-ehl-kye

"The Almighty Living God"

This is an old Hebrew name of God representing that aspect of the Divine that exists in the flow and tides of all things in life. It is this aspect of the Divine that awakens the strength to build new foundations within our lives.

Gabriel
gah-bree-ehl

"Angel of Hope, Illumination, and Love"

4. MUSIC AND MOVEMENT THERAPIES

We can use music and movement to amplify the strength of the muscles. With so many different kinds of muscles, there is no one exercise or series of movements that incorporates them all. What we can do, though, is incorporate general stretching for the major muscle groups of the body.

Stretching

Stretching the major muscles helps them retain elasticity, increasing their ability to perform. Stretching while playing Pachelbel's *Canon in D* or Brahm's *Symphony no. 2 in D Major* can be wonderful. It increases the blood flow and awakens the muscles. This is especially effective the first thing in the morning and is a wonderful "wake-me-up" to the muscles.

1. Begin with the feet, and gently flex and stretch the feet and work your way up the body slowly.

2. Stretch and flex most of the major muscle groups in turn—legs, hips, back, arms, neck, etc. Remember that stretching is slow and smooth. It

should never involve bouncing or pain.

3. Keep your breathing smooth and slow.

4. Perform the stretches while laying upon the floor or while standing— or both.

Learning Folk Dances

Learning dances associated with your own heritage heals and strengthens the muscles. Most colleges or community centers have folk dance classes. Learn a dance or two associated with your heritage.

Performing folk dances on a regular basis, once or twice a week, is a magnificent way to keep your muscles in harmony with soul memory. Some believe it helps strengthen cellular memory locked into the DNA structure. By performing this type of dance, you may truly be able to connect with our roots.

NOTES

Summary of Musical Guidelines
for Muscles

Chakra	Spleen
TONE	D, D sharp (*re*)
VOWEL	long o (*oh*)
MANTRAM	vam
INSTRUMENT	percussion, bass, brass
STYLE	rhapsodies, blues, African, Hispanic

Complimentary

Imbalance	Instrument	Key
general aches	percussion, brass	D
cramps	shakahachi, and Native American flutes	E flat
strain	woodwinds, soft percussion	D, E flat
swelling	—	G

Muscle Therapies

SOUNDS	COLORS	AROMAS
(*oh*)	pastel orange	lavender
—	yellow orange	lavender
—	peach	lavender, eucalyptus
(*eh, oh*)	pale blues	lavender, wisteria, camphor

*To believe in God or in a guiding force because
someone tells you to is the height of stupidity.
We are given senses to receive our information with.
With our own eyes we see, and with our skin we feel.
With our intelligence it is intended that we
understand. But each person must puzzle
it out for himself or herself.*[1]

---

[1] Sophie Burnham

Chapter 8

Music Therapies for the Nerves

All of our senses are linked to the nervous system. Taste, smell, hunger, pain, and many more are tied not only to their individual body systems, but to the entire nervous system as well. By studying the nervous system and our sensory organs, we can find the best clues to developing musical remedies for sensory or nervous imbalances.

Our Nervous System

The nervous system is like a telephone network, passing information to and from all the parts of the body. Through our nerves we are able to respond to changes in the environment inside and outside of us.

The brain and the spinal cord make up the central nervous system. The *brain* is the central control for thoughts, memories, intuition, senses, and perception. It has always had great symbolic significance as the seat of the soul and the doorway of spirit. The *spinal cord*, a cable from the brain, is made up of 31 pairs of nerves which branch off to stimulate

sensory and motor functions. The nerves to and from the spinal cord make up the *peripheral nervous system.* The *autonomic nervous system* sends and receives impulses to and from the vital organs on an involuntary basis.

OUR SENSE ORGANS

Our senses are closely tied to the nervous system as gateways to the brain.. The *sensory organs* are the receiving stations for impressions outside and within the brain, providing visual, auditory, tactile, and other data for the brain to work with.

The more senses involved in forming a mental picture, the more distinct and stronger the response from the nervous system. For our purposes, we will

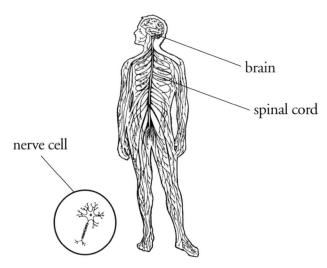

brain

spinal cord

nerve cell

focus upon the sense organs which most strongly influence the nervous system: the eyes, ears, and skin.

Eyes

Our eyes enable vision. Each eye is a nearly spherical hollow organ that is lined with a sensitive retina. The retina perceives light and color impulses, refracted by the lens. Inside the retina millions of nerve fibers pass the light impulse along the optic nerve to the brain, which coordinates the impulses into the image seen.

Ears

The ears are not only our organs for hearing, but also have a major role in our physical equilibrium. The ears pick up sound vibrations from the air, carrying them through the passageway to where they move against the eardrum, causing it to vibrate. These vibrations travel further into the ear and stimulate impulses within the nerves of the inner ear (cochlea). These impulses are translated into nerve signals and sent to the brain over the auditory nerve, where it is then translated and interpreted by the brain.

The Skin

The skin is another sensory organ with strong ties to the nervous system. Most people, when they think

of feeling in the skin, think of touch. This is only one of many skin sensations, including heat, cold, pressure, and pain. Skin sensations are registered in nerve endings all over the body. Nerve fibers carry them as impulses to the spinal cord and then on to the brain. The brain then interprets and registers the sensations.

Nerves and Sense Organ Problems

Physical problems related to the nervous system can be aggravated through unbalanced thought processes within various aspects of our life. We should examine how sensitive we are to the events within our life and whether we are responding appropriately to them.

For example, our eyes are sometimes referred to as the windows to the soul, and as such are the symbol of spiritual vision. Eye problems are often created or aggravated by distorted perceptions of events and situations within our life and can also be linked to how flexible we are in viewing ourselves and our lives.

Below are the more common emotions and mental attitudes that can irritate the nervous system or a sense organ's imbalances:

- anxiety,
- worry,
- doubt,
- fears,
- feeling misunderstood,
- shame,
- unsympathetic,
- isolation,
- stubbornness,
- feeling unprotected,
- feeling unloved, and
- irresponsibility.

If nervous system problems surface, they can provide an excellent opportunity to clarify important issues impacting upon our lives. With a little self-examination, we can discern the issues that may have contributed to or aggravated the condition. If nervous system problems arise, the following are good questions to ask:

Are we taking on too much?

Are we not doing enough?

Are we being too critical or are others around us?

Are we not communicating clearly?

Are we feeling misunderstood?

Are we viewing things through "rose colored glasses"?

Are we allowing others to disrupt our balance?

Are we feeling unworthy?

Are we taking responsibility for our lives?

Are we being insensitive? Are others around us?

Music Therapies for the Nerves

1. THERAPEUTIC MUSIC AND RHYTHM STYLES

A variety of musical styles can benefit and strengthen the nerves and sense organs of the body. Symphonies, big band music, and reggae are the most beneficial forms of music for the nervous system.

Symphonies

Symphonies are orchestral works, usually consisting of three or four movements and played by a full choir of strings, winds, and percussion. Because symphonies are performed with so many instruments, they have great potential for influencing many aspects of the nervous system.

The symphony is often said to have achieved its height in the 1700s with such composers as Haydn and Mozart. However, the symphony still holds its place today as the most popular form for the composer with serious things to say.

Big Band Music

The big band era of the 30s and 40s, arose from the style of earlier jazz bands such as Duke Ellington's.

This music's rhythms and combinations of instruments lends itself to strengthening and repairing an overwrought nervous system, particularly the swing music of the era.

Reggae

Reggae is another form of music that seems to calm the nervous system. This music arose out of the Jamaican and African sounds and is closely linked to the Rastaferian religion. Reggae's syncopated, soft, bouncy rhythms have a calming effect upon frayed nerves. Newborns and infants seem to respond well to it, and more and more parents are playing reggae to help soothe colic in their children.

Selected Music to Aid the Nervous System

The musical pieces in the table on the opposite page are beneficial to the nervous system.

MUSIC FOR THE NERVES

Composer	Work	Effect
Haydn	Symphony no. 85 (The Queen's Symphony)	strengthens entire nervous system, soothing and energizing at same time
Beethoven	Ninth Symphony	strengthens nerves; powerful tonic, particularly for brain imbalances
Schubert	—	calms and soothes; good for hypertension
Wagner	Parsifal	good for recovery situations; rebuilds sensitivities
Gershwin	Rhapsody in Blue	increases overall sensitivities without creating hypersensitivity
Ellington	Night Creature and other pieces	stimulates nerves; balances equilibrium; good for vision
Goodman	—	soothes and empowers nervous system; tempo stimulates senses

2. TONAL AND INSTRUMENTAL THERAPIES

The nervous system responds strongly to swing music and music that stimulates the crown and brow chakras.

Swing Music

The swing music of the '30s and '40s was much sweeter in tones than the earlier New Orleans jazz. Swing incorporates a rhythm designed to excite the listener, so it is powerful for rejuvenating a frayed or weakened nervous system.

Music to Stimulate the Crown Chakra

The crown chakra, tied to the subconscious mind, influences the skeletal and nervous systems of the body. The brow chakra also has an influence on the nervous system, as this is a center for balancing the hemispheres of the brain. Music that effects the crown chakra also effects the brow chakra.

Tones in the key of B or B flat (major and minor), in the scale of middle C, are most effective for the crown chakra. If using a more personal musical scale (See Appendix B), use the seventh interval in that scale.

The seventh in music awakens our senses, often hinting at a new sense of direction, as if new and unexpected doors are about to open. When we are relaxed, we feel as if a new threshold is opening for us.

The following musical selections are beneficial to stimulating the subconscious mind related to the crown chakra and also the brow chakra, aiding in balancing and healing the nervous system.

Remember to visualize the music surrounding you and then flowing into you through the crown chakra. See and feel it filling you and balancing the corresponding nervous system.

 Music for the Crown Chakra

Type	Composer	Work
key of B and B flat, both major and minor	Bach	Brandenburg Concerto in B Flat Major
	Louis Armstrong	Basin Street Blues
	Gershwin	Rhapsody in Blue
	Handel	Messiah
	Holst	The Planets
	Bob Marley	any music

3. Vocal Remedies for the Nerves

 We can employ individual vocal tones to interact with the nervous system as well as the crown and brow chakras. If you are unfamiliar with these methods, refer to the Vocal Remedies section in Chapter 2 for additional information.

Toning

 The vowel sounds and mantra in the table below will benefit the nervous system.

To enhance the effect, tone these sounds in their appropriate musical key. If using the generic musical scale of middle C, tone the sounds in B or B flat for the crown chakra and A or A sharp for the brow chakra. If using a more personal scale, use the seventh of your astrological scale (see Appendix B).

Chakra	Vowel Sound	Mantra
CROWN	long e (*ee*)	on (*ohm*)
BROW	long e (*ee*)	aum (*ahum*)

We can perform the toning by alternating the vowel sound and the mantrum for increased benefits. Doing this against the background of the appropriate music will even further enhance the effect.

Allow the toning to find its own rhythm. I recommend performing this against the background music of Haydn's *Symphony no. 85* or Beethoven's *Ninth Symphony.*

Affirming

Some dynamic affirmations can be used effectively with the nervous system, especially visualizing and performing the affirmations with feeling. Again, use background music to add to its benefits.

The following are sample affirmations that can be used to benefit the nervous system. Affirmations are always more powerful when we create them ourselves and when we can determine the metaphysical or hidden issues which may be creating our imbalance. When creating your affirmations, keep in mind the role of the nervous system: communication, sensing and perceptions.

I experience life fully and with joy!

I am at peace with all things!

I am understood and understanding of all!

I accomplish all that I do!

I work freely and joyfully!
I see and experience all clearly!
I am confident in all I do!
I am connected to all things!
I am in touch with the joys of life!
All is clear and loving within my life!

NOTES

WORDS OF POWER

Jehovah Elohim
yah-hoh-vah-eh-loh-heem

"The Divine Perfection
through Creation"

That aspect of the Divine which helps us
to understand our own
perfection and the healing ability
through relaxed creativity.

Eheieh
eh-huh-yeh

"I am that I am"

The name for the deepest aspect of the
Divine that we have access to, that aspect
of the Divine that is an ever-present fact
within out lives.

Tzaphkiel
zahf-kye-ehl

"Angel of Comfort and Understanding"

Ratziel
rahtz-eye-ehl

"Angel of Hidden and
Concealed Things"

4. MUSIC AND MOVEMENT THERAPIES

For the nervous system, there are a variety of movements that can enhance the musical therapies. Any slow, smooth, and calming movement serves to relax and enhance the musical effects. Because of this, I typically recommend yoga postures.

Yoga Postures

The benefits of yoga upon the endocrine and the nervous system are well documented "Yogic postures help to strengthen the endocrine system through exercise, and also bring the emotions under control through concentration and relaxation."[2]

Yoga asanas can be combined with the therapeutic music we have chosen to enhance and strengthen any body system. Some lend themselves more to the particular system than others.

The Sun Salutation, an exercise for the circulatory system described in Chapter 3, is also very balancing to the entire body, including its nervous system. By performing it with the music for the nervous or glandular system and focusing upon that system while performing it, we increase the benefits.

---

[2] Swami Vishnudevananda, *The Complete Illustrated Book of Yoga* (New York: Pocket Books, 1960), p. 65.

This is an exercise that should be savored. It is wonderful to the body and the mind. Take your time and enjoy the stretching. Know that as you do the movement, you are relaxing all of the nerve fibers of the spine and as a result, all of them throughout the body.

You can increase the benefits of this exercise by performing it against the backdrop of any of the music listed in this chapter as beneficial to the nervous system.

Any movement or exercise performed slowly with great stretching along the spine can relax and balance the nervous system. The traditional cat pose or stretch is wonderful to perform with music for the nerves is the traditional cat pose or stretch.

The Cat Pose

The cat posture instills flexibility and relaxation to both the body and mind. In performing it, try to mimic the stretching and yawning antics of cats.

1. Get down on all fours.

2. Breathe slowly and smoothly, taking a moment to allow the music to envelop you.

3. Exhale. As you exhale, slowly stretch the arms forward on the floor while lowering the head and upper body toward the floor, keeping the buttocks up.

4. Inhale. As you inhale, relax into this posture, visualizing yourself as a cat stretching.

5. Stretch slowly and comfortably, reaching forward a little further each time and holding.

   As a variation, you can lower the buttocks to the heels and stretch forward from this position as well.

6. Upon reaching the farthest stretch, hold the position.

7. Slowly rise up again to all fours and arch your back upwards, dropping the head down.

8. Lower the back to the original all-fours position, and repeat the cat stretch forward. Perform this for about ten minutes.

Summary of Musical Guidelines
for Nerves

Chakra	Brow	Crown
TONE	A, A sharp (*la*)	B (*ti*)
VOWEL	long e (*ee*)	long e (*ee*)
MANTRAM	aum	om
INSTRUMENT	strings, violins, cello, harp, acoustic guitar	strings, violins, piano
STYLE	symphony	jazz (traditional)

Complimentary

IMBALANCE	INSTRUMENT	KEY
Alzheimer	strings, violins	E, B
ear problems	reggae music, harpsichord	G, G sharp
eye problems	strings, violins	A
general conditions	Baroque style strings	musical scale
hypertension	strings	A, B flat
skin	orchestra	musical scale

Nerve Therapies

SOUNDS	COLORS	AROMAS
(*aw, ee*)	violet, indigo; combined opposites (red & blue, yellow & indigo)	rosemary, sage, thyme, violet
(*eh, uh*)	sky blue, blue & orange, turquoise	wisteria, eucalyptus
(*ee*)	blue, indigo	eucalyptus, rosemary, pennyroyal, honeysuckle
—	colors of rainbow	lilac, lavender, narcissus
(*ee*)	indigo, violet	eucalyptus, myrrh
—	pink	lilac, wisteria

*The creative attitude should remain with us always
and be the touchstone by which we gauge our actions
in the world. It is a feeling of self-confidence,
a recognition of the Divine within each of us...
It is part of the process of evolution.*[1]

---

[1] Nik Douglas and Penny Slinger, *Sexual Secrets* (New York: Destiny Books, 1979), p. 19.

Chapter 9

Music Therapies for Reproduction

For most people, reproduction involves mating to create offspring. However, reproduction can also refer to cell replacement within the different systems. Since the reproductive organs involve glands, there is a direct connection to the endocrine system. Reproduction involves the sexual organs, but there is much more to the reproductive process than science understands, even today. For our purposes, the focus of this chapter will be upon the sexual organs and the reproductive process.

In most ancient traditions, there was a great mysticism surrounding sexuality. Producing offspring was more than a physical act. There was a mystical aspect and it was honored. Sexual energy and the reproductive process were considered a reflection of our most creative essence. They were tied to the very life force within us, what used to be called the *kundalini*, with physical and spiritual elements that needed to be understood. The male organs often symbolized the activating force within nature, while the female organs symbolized the receptive and formative force.

Male Reproductive Organs

In males, the *testes* and the *penis* are the primary reproductive organs. Although the penis is often considered the primary male reproductive organ, it is actually the testes. Housed within the *scrotum,* the testes produce the male sex cells, the sperm. The testes also generate the male hormone testosterone which is important for the development of male sexual characteristics. The penis is actually more of an outer reflection or symbol of what the testes do: an organ of production and delivery.

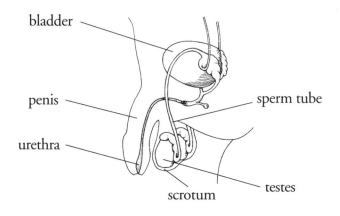

MALE REPRODUCTIVE ORGANS

Problems with the male sexuality are often aggravated by how creativity and productivity are expressed or interpreted by the individual.

Female Reproductive Organs

In females, the primary organs or reproduction are ovaries, vagina, and mammary glands. Like the testes, the ovaries are responsible for the production of the female sex cells and several female hormones. The vagina is the external opening that serves as the receptacle for the male sperm and as the birth canal.

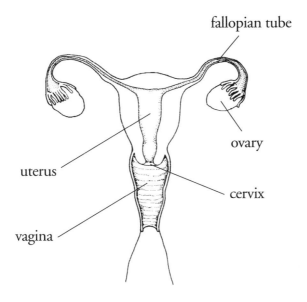

Female Reproductive Organs

The mammary glands are actually modified skin glands that produce and secrete milk.

In every society, the mammary glands have been, and still are, symbols of nourishment, mothering, and sexuality. Problems with female sexuality often are aggravated by issues revolving around expression of creativity and nourishment.

Problems with the Reproductive System

The reproductive process and its various organs are too complicated to cover within a work such as this. But any problem with sex and the reproduction organs may reflect upon issues surrounding how we express our creativity in life. A number of the following emotions and mental attitudes are likely to create problems with the reproductive system:

- disapproval of self or others,
- lack of creative activity,
- non-acceptance,
- anger at mate,
- stifled creativity,
- conflicted thoughts on sexuality,
- shame,
- lack of emotional nourishment,
- immaturity,

- issues surrounding grief,
- nursing old wounds, and
- smothering.

If reproductive or sexual problems surface, they provide a wonderful opportunity to clarify issues within our life. With a little self-examination, we can discern the issues that may have contributed to the imbalance. If reproductive problems arise, the following questions could be asked:

How fertile and creative do we feel in life?

Are we feeling stifled in our creativity?

Are we stifling others' creativity?

Are we nursing old wounds and not letting them go?

Are we taking time to rejuvenate ourselves?

Are we able to express our sexuality freely and comfortably?

Are we behaving immaturely and failing to take responsibility?

Do we have conflicting thoughts about our sexual needs and desires?

Music Therapies for Reproduction

1. THERAPEUTIC MUSIC AND RHYTHM STYLES

 There are probably more varieties of music for the reproductive system than for any other. Individual tastes in music seem to play a stronger role with this system than the others. Everyone seems to have their own opinion as to what stimulates or arouses them. For some, it is the romantic classics, for others it is rock and roll, and for still others it is the blues. Because of personal taste, it is more difficult to musically define this area.

Ballads, Blues, Hispanic, and African Rhythms

For the most part, the blues, African, and Hispanic rhythms are a great stimulus to sexual energies,[2] along with most tribal rhythms as well. Romantic ballads also have a great impact as well. In a more classical area, opera, although for many an acquired taste, can be a wonderful stimulus.

---

[2] Refer to Chapter 5 for more information on the blues. Refer to Chapter 7 for additional information on Hispanic rhythms.

Ballets

Of all the styles of music, ballet music, written for dance, seems to lend itself strongly to music therapy for the reproductive system.

The music usually has strong rhythms with clear cadences and is meant to be danced to, symbolic of the dance of life and all aspects of it, including sexuality.

Dance has been used to arouse sexuality and to awaken fertility. There have been dances for healing, and even for destruction, and all of these themes can be been found within the music of ballet. Ballet music has many themes and can be a wonderful tool for balancing and healing the reproductive system.

Selected Music to Aid the Reproduction System

The pieces of music shown in the table on the following two pages are some of the most beneficial for the reproductive system.

MUSIC FOR THE REPRODUCTION SYSTEM

Composer	Work	Effect
Handel	Water Music	benefits entire reproductive system; heals and soothes, especially throughout pregnancy
Bach	Jesu, Joy of Man's Desiring	benefits all aspects of reproduction, pregnancy, childbirth; opens blockages; good for diseases of sexual organs
Mendelssohn	Violin Concertos	eases relationship problems; opens communications
Gluck	Dance of the Blessed Spirits	good when attempting pregnancy and in childbirth
Stravinsky	The Firebird	romantic and stimulating; rejuvenates all aspects of sexuality and reproduction

MUSIC FOR THE REPRODUCTION SYSTEM (CONT.)

Composer	Work	Effect
Beethoven	Moonlight Sonata	stirring and romantic; stimulates feeling of nature and compatibility of couples
Saint-Saens	Bacchanalia from Samson and Delilah	passionate and flowing, moves from sexuality to romance; puts fires back in relationships
Wagner	Tristan and Isolde	heals and strengthens; beneficial for those struggling for pregnancy
Tchaikovsky	Sleeping Beauty	strengthens reproduction; heals entire system and all organs

2. TONAL AND INSTRUMENTAL THERAPIES

 Several tonal and instrumental therapies benefit the reproductive system. In the Eastern tradition, the sex organs are associated with the spleen or second chakra, and to some degree the base chakra. As discussed in Chapter 7, the spleen chakra is a link to that level of the subconscious mind that controls the muscular system and influences the eliminative system. There is also a connection to the heart chakra which is a level of the subconscious that influences the breasts.

In a musical scale, these two centers form a natural third. Musically, this is a simple and uncluttered chord, a harmony of resonance. For those with reproductive problems, there should be some examination of the harmony between sexual passion and the passion of the heart, a reminder that the greatest sex is that in which there is love.

For those with problems in the breast area of the body, working with fourths can be beneficial. In music, a fourth is used to announce something new, an entrance. Working with fourths can help the individual move into new health. In the generic musical scale of middle C, this would be music written in the key of F or F sharp, both major and minor.

If working with a more personal musical scale, use the tone for the heart chakra. Refer to Appendix B for additional information.

If focusing only on the sex organs, individually or together, music in the key of D or E can be beneficial. If using the personal musical scale, refer to the second chakra for the key notes.

Percussion, Strings, and Strong Musical Rhythms

Celebrational music of all traditions can be used to stimulate the base chakra as well as music in the key of C, both major and minor. We can use all blues music and most rhapsodies to stimulate the spleen chakra as well as music in the key of D and E flat, both major and minor.

Percussion instruments and strong rhythms are beneficial for stimulating sexuality. Violins and strings are also very beneficial. Together, in orchestrated form, they can create wonderful dance music that can be powerfully healing.

The following musical selections are beneficial for stimulating those levels of the subconscious mind and their corresponding chakras in balancing and healing the reproductive system.

MUSIC FOR THE
BASE, SPLEEN, AND HEART CHAKRAS

Chakra	Composer	Work
BASE *key of C, both major and minor* *celebrational music of all traditions*	Saint-Saëns Beethoven	Symphony no. 3 in C Major Fifth Symphony
SPLEEN *key of D, E flat, both major and minor* *all blues music; most rhapsodies*	Beethoven Stravinsky	Creatures of Prometheus The Firebird; The Rite of Spring
HEART *key of F, F sharp, both major and minor*	Beethoven Chopin Tshaikovsky Gounod	Symphony no. 6, (Pastorale); La Sylphide Etude Nutcracker Valpurga's Night

3. Vocal Remedies for Reproduction

Employing vocal tones helps us to participate more actively with our own healing. Toning, chanting, and affirming are wonderful ways of affecting the reproductive system. If you are unfamiliar with toning, refer to the Vocal Remedies section in Chapter 2.

We can further enhance the benefits of toning, chanting, and such by listening to music beneficial to the reproductive system in the background while performing our toning, chanting or affirming. Some excellent music beneficial for the reproductive system are Ravel's *Bolero*, Tschaikovsky's *Sleeping Beauty*, and Stravinsky's *The Firebird*.

Other ways of vocalizing to influence the body include reading out loud or storytelling. A growing number of couples are reading romantic poetry and romance novels to each other to stimulate passion and renew their sexual energies. A little exploration of this within one's own life might bring some wonderful surprises.

Toning

The vowel sounds and mantras found in the table at the bottom of this page are beneficial to the reproductive system.

For the greatest benefit to the reproductive system, tone both the vowels and the mantras. To enhance their overall effects, tone them in the appropriate key:

- C for the base chakra,
- D and E flat for the spleen chakra, and
- F for the heart chakra.

Again, feel free to use your own more personal musical scale, and do not be afraid to experiment to discover what works best for you individually.

Chakra	Vowel Sound	Mantra
BASE	long u (*oo*)	lam (*lahm*)
SPLEEN	long o (*oh*)	vam (*vahm*)
HEART	long a (*ay*)	yam (*yahm*)

Affirming

Affirmations are a wonderful way to influence the reproductive system. Below are a series of affirmations that I have used with clients.

I am creative in life!

I am fertile and productive in all I do!

I am fertile in all I do!

I am creative and productive in all I do!

I find joy and fulfillment in all I create!

I am free of the past and in the flow of life!

I embrace my own sexuality!

I am receptive to new blessings!

My life is born anew each day!

I am nurtured and nourished by all of life!

You might also want to create your own affirmations. If you do so, keep in mind the emotional and mental issues in your life that may be aggravating the condition. Also keep in mind the significance and role of the reproductive system.

WORDS OF POWER

Adonai Ha Aretz
ah-doh-nye-hah-
ah-retz

"Lord of the Earth"

Aspect of the Divine influencing forces
of birth and growth available to us
through nature, whether it is
the nature of the world or the nature
of ourselves.
Believed to influence our
physical lives the most.

Shaddai El Chai
shah-dye-ehl-kye

"The Almighty Living God"

Helps us understand the Divine plane
within our lives and the "machinery"
that helps us with its fulfillment,
particularly the machinery
of reproduction.

Sandalphon
san-dahl-fawn

"Angel of Prayer and Birth"

Hanael
hahn-ah-ehl

"Angel of Love, Harmony, Creativity,
and Sexuality"

4. MUSIC AND MOVEMENT THERAPIES

A variety of movements and exercises are beneficial for the reproductive system. Taoism and tantric traditions teach the importance of the healing and spiritual aspects of sexuality and can provide a wonderful starting point for anyone wishing to explore this realm more closely. In this book, the focus will be on simple movements effective for energizing and strengthening the reproductive system.

The Sun Salutation (described in Chapter 3) and the Pelvic Circles (described in Chapter 5) are just two of the exercises discussed in earlier chapters that can be beneficial to the reproductive system.

The Turtle Posture

The primary movements of what is sometimes referred to as the turtle posture is very beneficial to the reproductive systems and is easy to learn.

The turtle has had great significance in many societies and is often the symbol of sexuality:

> In Nigeria, the turtle was a symbol of the female sex organs and sexuality. To the Native Americans, it was

associated with the lunar cycle, menstruation and the power of female energies.[3]

In Eastern traditions, the turtle was an animal that could link the heavens with the earth, symbolic of linking the male and female. Its shell was a symbol of the heavens and its squarish underside representative of the Earth, able to invoke the blessings of heaven on earth, particularly through the birth of a child (the spirit manifesting upon the earth).

In other traditions, it was a symbol of the male organ and sexuality, the head coming out of the shell symbolizing the phallus.

Playing appropriate slow, sensual background music can make these movements even more effective.

1. Draw the knee up, hugging the leg next to the body, and arch the back, stretching (Figure A and Figure B).

Repeat this slowly with each leg five to six times.

Figure A

Figure B

---

[3] Ted Andrews, *Animal-Speak* (St. Paul, Minnesota: Llewellyn Publications, 1993), p. 364.

By drawing the knees up and by stretching the body at the same time, the abdominal muscles are strengthened, in turn stimulating the inner sexual fires.

Figure C

2. Get into a seated position upon the floor. The soles of the feet should be touching and the knees as open as is comfortable (Figure C).

As the music you have chosen plays in the background, with your elbows resting upon the upper thighs, draw the heels of your feet in toward the groin area.

Figure D

3. Slowly begin caressing and massaging the area of the legs between the knees and the sex organs (Figure D).

This stimulates the energies and balances them.

4. Remain seated on the floor and imagine yourself as a turtle.

Let the music help you with this.

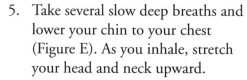

Figure E

5. Take several slow deep breaths and lower your chin to your chest (Figure E). As you inhale, stretch your head and neck upward.

    You will feel the neck pull up and the shoulders should relax down.

6. Raise your head and chin, tilting them up and back, as if looking at the ceiling (Figure F). Your shoulders will rise and you will exhale.

    It is O.K. to keep the eyes closed through this. Keep the movements slow—like a turtle.

Figure F

7. Repeat steps 5 through 6 ten to twelve times.

8. Sit still for a few moments. Imagine yourself as the turtle. Keep in mind all of the sexual and reproductive significance of the turtle as you do.

    Know that as you focus upon the image, your system becomes strong, healthy and fertile.

SUMMARY OF MUSICAL GUIDELINES
FOR REPRODUCTION

Chakra	Base	Spleen	Heart
TONE	C, C sharp (*do*)	D, D sharp (*re*)	F, F sharp (*fa*)
VOWEL	long u (*oo*)	long o (*oh*)	long a (*ay*)
MANTRAM	lam	vam	yam
INSTRU-MENT	bass, percussion	percussion, bass, brass	strings
STYLE	blues, African	Hispanic, African, blues	ballet

Complimentary

IMBALANCE	INSTRUMENT	KEY
breasts	harps, cello	F
cramps (menstrual)	soft percussion, woodwinds	D, D sharp
menstrual (general problems)	soft percussion	C, F
sexual energy (too much or too little)	percussions, bass	C, C sharp

Reproductive Therapies

SOUNDS	COLORS	AROMAS
(*ay*)	pink, violet	rose, lilac, patchouli
(*oh*)	peach	pennyroyal, hyacinth, chamomile*
(*oo, ay*)	soft reds, blue-green	pennyroyal, hyacinth, patchouli
(*oo*)	reds, fire tones	cinnamon, patchouli

---

* Caution should be taken when using chamomile as it is a member of the ragweed family. Some people may be sensitive to or have an allergic reaction to it.

We have all experienced the direct link
between our breathing and the way we feel
physically and emotionally.
We speak of a sigh of relief, of gasping in horror,
of holding our breath in anticipation,
of being breathless with excitement.[1]

---

[1] Nancy Zi, *The Art of Breathing* (New York: Bantam Books, 1986), pp. 8-9.

Chapter 10

Music Therapies for Respiration

Air and breathing have had great significance throughout the world. Air has been symbolic of the heavens and of the intellect. Breathing—proper breathing—is the way many believe we can learn to move between the earth and the heavens. Breath is life.

We live through breathing, and whatever air is blowing around us is what we take in. It has the ability to affect us physically and spiritually. Learning to control what we take into our life is part of what used to be called the "initiation of air" and part of why breathing has had such a mystical aspect to it.

Our Respiratory System

Our respiratory system, through breathing, takes in oxygen and eliminates carbon dioxide, exchanging gases throughout the body. Its primary organs are the lungs, sinuses, nostrils, and trachea. Our focus here will be upon the functions of the lungs, the nose, and the sinuses.

The *lungs* are the primary organs of the respiratory system, enabling us to take in oxygen and to exhale carbon dioxide. The lungs allow the body's cells to absorb oxygen for their own benefits. The taking in of breath has a great mystical aspect. Some traditions believe that inhaling and exhaling reflects our own process of evolution, including how well we are integrating life and spirit through normal everyday circumstances.

The *nose* serves a vital function in breathing, cleansing and warming the air we breathe so that the lungs can absorb and transfer it more easily. The nose also, through the olfactory sense, enables us to smell. Because of these two functions, the nose has often been symbolic of the ability to discriminate, reflecting what we allow ourselves to take into our lives.

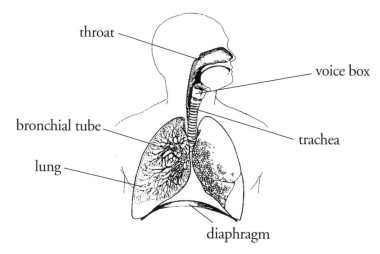

The *sinuses* are the air cavities within the head. In conjunction with the nostrils, they help to warm the air we breathe. They also assist us in hearing, serving as sound chambers for the voice. When the sinuses are clogged or irritated, we may be allowing things in our life to clog and irritate us as well.

Respiratory Problems

Respiration is essential for life. Problems with breathing often center around primary issues of life and whether we feel worthy. They can also reflect an inability to take in and express life effectively. A number of emotions and mental attitudes that can irritate respiratory problems include the following:

- feeling unworthy,
- melancholy,
- stubbornness,
- surrendering attitudes,
- dogmatic attitudes in us or those close to us,
- guilt,
- suppressing emotions,
- one-sidedness,
- feeling smothered,
- indiscriminate behaviors,

- irritability with self or others, and
- impatience.

Lungs that work fully and strong will more easily filter out the disease-causing agents that we might encounter in the air around us on a daily basis. Test the balance of your lungs. If your exhalation is longer than the inhalation, there is imbalance—more air is going out than is coming in. Are you a mouth breather or a nose breather? You should breathe through the nose, as the nose serves as a filter.

If respiratory problems surface, it gives us an opportunity to face issues that may be connected to them. With a little self-examination, we can usually discern what issues may have contributed to the imbalance by asking the following questions:

Do we feel unworthy to live the life we are?

Are we feeling guilty about our life or something in it?

Are we suppressing emotions?

Is there an equal exchange in our life?

Are we giving as much as taking?

Are we irritating others or allowing them to do so to us?

Is our life congested with too much activity?

Are we feeling unrecognized and unappreciated?

Music Therapies for Respiration

1. Therapeutic Music And Rhythm Styles

A number of musical styles can be beneficial to the respiratory system. Among these are reggae, ragtime, big band music, and music of the Romantic Period.

Reggae and Ragtime

Reggae, as mentioned earlier, grew from Jamaican and African roots. Its syncopated rhythm is calming and relaxing, facilitating expression. See Chapter 8 for additional information on reggae.

Ragtime, a style of piano jazz, originated in the honky-tonk cafes of the 1890s. Ragtime gets its name from classical melodies that were "given a ragtime treatment in a style known as 'ragging the classics.'"[2]

Big Band Music

The big band sounds, particularly the swing music of the '30s and '40s, with its driving rhythm and strong harmonies, stimulate the respiratory system, can ease tightness and congestion in the lungs.

---

[2] Norman Lloyd, *The Golden Encyclopedia of Music* (New York: Golden Press, 1968), p. 453.

Classical Romantic Music and Minuets

Classical music of the Romantic Period (late 1700s to early 1900s) provides some wonderful pieces to stimulate and open the respiratory system. Its expressiveness and feeling enable the listener to breathe and feel the music deeply.

The minuet, also from the Romantic Period, is one of the most beneficial for all respiratory conditions. It was the most popular form of court dances of the mid 1600s to 1800.

Both the music and dance of a minuet were graceful and formal. The dancers would move in rhythmic harmony, performing dainty retreats and approaches (a high step and a balanced pause), guided by the music. It almost mimics soft gentle breathing, in and out like a dance of breath. Because of this, dancing a minuet is very beneficial for restoring normal breathing patterns.

Selected Music to Aid the Respiratory System

The table on following two pages lists musical selections beneficial to the respiratory system

MUSIC FOR THE RESPIRATORY SYSTEM

Composer	Work	Effect
Joplin	Maple Leaf Rag	syncopated, jerky rhythms smooth and ease labored breathing
Stravinsky	Piano Rag Music	opens congestion, eases labored breathing
Ellington	Mood Indigo	soothes respiratory distress, eases labored breathing
Mahler	Symphony no. 4 in G Major	soothes and heals most respiratory problems; eases emotional tightness of lungs
Handel	Water Music	soothes and heals sinus imbalances; eases lung congestion
Wagner	Ride of Valkyries	releases anger over life that may be congesting respiration

MUSIC FOR THE RESPIRATORY SYSTEM (CONT.)

Composer	Work	Effect
Brahms	Liebeslieder Waltzes	releases emotions that may be aggravating the condition; opens new breathing, physically and emotionally
	Lullaby	eases breathing difficulties; especially effective at night for more peaceful rest
Beethoven	Minuet in G	restores breathing patterns to normal; calms children in asthmatic attacks
Mozart	Symphony no. 40 in G Minor	calms respiratory distress; opens the lungs and facilitates deeper breaths

2. TONAL AND INSTRUMENTAL THERAPIES

The throat chakra directs the level of the subconscious for respiration. The heart center, discussed earlier, also has some impact upon respiration.

In Eastern traditions, the throat center is tied to the function of the throat, ears, lungs (particularly the upper lobes), sinuses, and all aspects of respiration. The throat chakra is associated with our ability to express, emotionally and physically. The inability to do so may reflect imbalances at that level and may intensify respiratory problems.

Orchestra and Band Music

Orchestra and band music incorporating strings and percussion are beneficial for the respiratory system. This is why playing the piano can help heal respiratory imbalances. By striking the piano's keys, we combine strings and a percussion effect. Woodwinds instruments are also beneficial because playing them exercises the lungs and improves breathing.[3]

---

[3] Mark Bricklin, *The Practical Encyclopedia of Natural Healing* (Emmaus, Pennsylvania: Rodale Press, 1983), p. 343. This article cites a study that is specific to children with asthma.

Ted Andrews   231

Music in the Key of G and G sharp

Playing music in the key of F sharp and G can benefit the respiratory system. In the generic scale of middle C, this is a natural fifth, an interval of movement and power. Composers use it to awaken a feeling of new life and rebirth. It opens us to a breath of fresh air. If using a more personal scale (as mentioned in Appendix B), use music in the key associated with your astrological sign's throat center.

Selected Music to Stimulate the Throat Chakra

The following musical selections are beneficial for stimulating the throat chakra in balancing and healing the respiratory system.

 MUSIC FOR THE THROAT CHAKRA

Type	Composer	Work
key of G, G sharp, both major and minor	Beethoven	Moonlight Sonata
	Schubert	Unfinished Symphony
all minuets, especially piano and harpsichord piece	Chopin	Prelude in A Major

3. VOCAL REMEDIES FOR RESPIRATION

 Toning, chanting, and affirming methods quite often have a much more beneficial impact on respiratory problems than other systems because breath is such an integral part of vocalizing. Refer to the Vocal Remedies section of Chapter 2 for additional information on the toning process.

Toning

 The vowel sounds and mantras in the table at the bottom of this page are beneficial for the respiratory system.

To enhance the effects of toning, chanting, and affirming, play beneficial music in the background. Remember to keep the music soft and nonintrusive. Allow your toning and chanting to find its own rhythm.

Chakra	Vowel Sound	Mantra
HEART	long a (*ay*)	yam (*yahm*)
THROAT	short e (*eh*)	ham (*hahm*)

Working With Asthmatic Children

There is a beneficial method for using the vowel sound and breath work with asthmatic children to help them head off an asthma episode. Whenever I teach workshops on sound therapy, I teach this technique. With asthma, the difficulty is not getting air into the lungs; but rather getting the air out. The air has become trapped by the bronchioles in the lungs. By combining a hard sigh (which forces air out) with the vowel sound of long A, we can help to restore balance and prevent the episode from becoming worse.

With smaller children, rest your hands gently on the chest and back. This is comforting to the child and will help prevent the panic of not being able to breathe properly from worsening the condition. Perform the sighing breath with the child, sighing out the long A sound "ayyyy." The sighing breath forces the air out, and the long A sound simultaneously works to balance and relax the lungs.

Asthmatic children also seem to respond well to the music and rhythm of soft minuets. Play such music at night while they go to sleep to help them sleep more deeply and more trouble-free.

Affirming

Affirmations can be very helpful when toning. Again, they are particularly effective when we can determine the metaphysical effects or hidden issues behind the actual imbalance. The following are some beneficial affirmations:

I am at peace with life!

I breathe in joy in all I do!

I am nurtured and loved!

There is a joyful flow of blessings in my life!

I embrace life fully!

My spirit breathes freely!

I breathe in life with joy!

I am worthy of joy in life!

I am free to enjoy life freely and completely!

If you are creating your own affirmations, keep in mind the role and function of the respiratory system: learning to control what we breathe into our lives.

WORDS OF POWER

Jehovah Aloah
Va Daath
yah-hoh-vah-ay-
loh-ah-vuh-dawth

"The Divine Made Manifest
through the Mind"

This is that aspect of the Divine
closest to the heart,
enabling our thoughts and
words to manifest physically.

Jehovah Elohim
yah-hoh-vah-eh-
loh-heem

"Divine Perfection through Creation"

This aspect of the Divine is associated
with creative expression, particularly
vocal expression. Breath is necessary to
speak, and thus is essential to being a
creative, healthy individual.

Raphael
rah-fah-ehl

"Angel of Beauty, Brightness,
and Healing"

Gabriel
gah-bree-ehl

"Angel of Comfort"

4. MUSIC AND MOVEMENT THERAPIES

Movement to aid in respiration should be gentle and peaceful, stretching and relaxing the lungs and the diaphragm muscles The exercise that follows is adapted from Taoist techniques for working with the lungs. Keep in mind that exercising the lungs is essential to overall health. Since I have a predisposition toward lung problems, I take extra care to exercise my lungs regularly to try to prevent unnecessary imbalances.

The lung exercise that follows is simple but very effective. As you perform this exercise, visualize and feel fresh air filling your lungs. See and feel the lung tissues vitalized, energized, healed, and balanced. To enhance the effects, perform this exercise with music appropriate for the respiratory system.

In the beginning, repeat this exercise approximately 7-10 times. You may even wish to take a breath between cycles, but eventually, you will develop a rhythm that will make that unnecessary.

1. Begin by standing straight with your feet shoulder width apart. Allow your shoulders to relax down and let the arms hang loose at your side.

2. Exhale to remove all of the air from your lungs and then clasp your hands behind your back (Figure A).

3. Now slowly inhale, expanding your lungs and pushing your clasped hands out and away from your back.

Figure A

4. Exhale, unclasping your hands and slowly bringing your arms forward, circling them slowly with the exhalation, over your head and back to your side (Figure B).

5. Clasp your hands behind your back again and inhale.

6. Repeat the circling motion with the exhalation.

Figure B

Summary of Musical Guidelines
for Respiration

Chakra	Heart	Throat
TONE	F (*fa*)	G (*sol*)
VOWEL	long a (*ay*)	short e (*eh*)
MANTRAM	yam	harn
INSTRUMENT	strings and woodwinds combined	cellos
STYLE	Baroque, Renaissance	Renaissance, Romantic

Complimentary

Imbalance	Instrument	Key
allergies	violins, bagpipes	A, B flat
asthma	flutes	F, G
bronchitis	flute, violin combinations	F sharp
colds, chest	flutes, strings	F, G
colds, head	percussion, soft orchestra	C
congestion (lung)	bands, orchestra	F sharp, G
congestion, (nasal)	harp	C, A
sinus	strings	A, A sharp

Respiration Therapies

Sounds	Colors	Aromas
(*ee*)	indigo; red and blue combined	eucalyptus, gardenia,
(*ay, eh*)	turquoise	eucalyptus, bay
(*ay*)	blue-greens	bay, eucalyptus
(*ay, eh*)	turquoise, sky blue	eucalyptus, jasmine*
(*oo*)	red, red-orange	eucalyptus
(*ay*)	turquoise	eucalyptus
(*oo, ee*)	red-orange	cinnamon, eucalyptus, bay
(*ee*)	red and blue combined	bay, eucalyptus

* Jasmine frequently stimulates the mucous membranes and may result in coughing up mucous throughout the night, along with stimulating sinus drainage which could interfere with sleep. Caution is advised.

*In order to accomplish anything, we have
to have faith in ourselves. Very few people have faith
in themselves. They like to put faith in other people
and then they are shattered when other people
do not live up to their expectations.
Have faith in the power of God
which lives in you.*[1]

---

[1] Hanna Kroeger, *New Dimensions in Healing Yourself* (Boulder, Colorado: Chapel of Miracles, 1991), p. 137.

Chapter 11

Music Therapies for the Skeleton

The skeletal system is our foundation, comprised of all the bones in the body, including the teeth. It also incorporates the minor cartilage as well. The bones, our body's framework, serve a variety of functions, helping us to move, forming blood, protecting soft tissues within the body, and serving as a reservoir for the body's minerals.

Our Skeletal System

The *bones*, as our structure and our support, have in the past been symbols for resurrection and a strong foundation. Our bone structure has been likened to the Tree of Life. The different kinds of bones serve a variety of purposes. Examining the individual bones or groupings and their role within the body can assist us in determining emotional issues that are more likely to aggravate skeletal imbalances.

The ankle bones often reflect the amount of support we have for our movement or direction in life. The feet enable us to balance and to move forward.

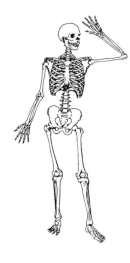

As the foundation of the skeletal system, they often reflect our success in making moves. The bones of the arms may reflect issues about what we are embracing in life. Bones of the hands and fingers may reveal how we touch and handle the issues and circumstances within our life.

The hip bones, some of the strongest and largest in the body, work to support and balance the body, particularly in forward movement. They can often reflect how much confidence we have in our movements in life as well as our overall balance.

SYMBOLIC MEANING OF OUR BONES

Bones	Reflection
ANKLE	support we have for life's direction
ARMS	how we embrace life
FEET	success in making moves
HANDS AND FINGERS	our handling of life's circumstances
HIP	confidence in our life's movements and overall balance
JOINT	flexibility in life

The bones around joints are also significant. *Joints* facilitate the movement and use of our limbs, helping us to change directions and perform activities with greater ease. They reflect our flexibility in life.

Problems With Our Bones

Since our bones are our support system, any problems with the skeletal system can reflect issues revolving around the kind of support we have or are giving within our lives. The following are some of the primary emotions likely to aggravate skeletal problems or imbalances within the body:

- feeling misunderstood,
- unsympathetic,
- lack of tenderness,
- stubbornness,
- inflexibility,
- fear of the future,
- poor self-worth,
- insecurity,
- hypocrisy, and
- feeling vulnerable.

If skeletal problems surface, they can provide an opportunity to clarify issues that may be affecting our life. With a little self-examination, we can discern what may have contributed to or caused the imbalance. If skeletal problems arise, the following are some good questions to ask:

Are we feeling vulnerable and exposed?

Are we supported in our activities?

Are we supportive of others in their activities?

Are we being inflexible?

Are others around us inflexible?

Are we taking on too much responsibility?

Are we too rigid in our thoughts?

Are we afraid to move on and try new things?

Are we feeling unbalanced?

Music Therapies for the Skeleton

1. THERAPEUTIC MUSIC AND RHYTHM STYLES

Several styles of music are therapeutic for the skeletal system. These include jazz improvisation and two more classical styles of music—impressionistic and impromptu.

Jazz Improvisation

Jazz is one of the most beneficial types of music for the skeletal system. There are a variety of jazz styles ranging from boogie-woogie to swing, from bop to barrel house, from ragtime to blues to New Orleans.

The heart of all jazz is rhythm, a bounce or swing because of its syncopated beats. Jazz is also defined by its improvisation. Traditional jazz is much more beneficial to the skeletal system than jazz fusion.

Traditional jazz improvisation occurs over a figured bass, and calls for variations over a set harmonic plan, whereas jazz fusion does not always follow this pattern. Good improvisation occurs over rhythms, chords, melodies, and instruments just as in symphonic music. Improvisation typically involves the foundation of the figured bass and the music's

rhythms. This gives jazz a symbolic connection to the skeletal system, since our skeletal system is our base.

Impressionism

Impressionism is a more classical style of music that is beneficial for the skeletal system. Impressionism is a term more often associated with French artists such as Monet, Renoir, and Van Gogh; it reached its highest point in the late 1800s. These artists tried to give an impression of something seen just for a moment. Musical impressionists such as Debussy and Ravel attempted the same thing.

Impressionistic music is full of contrasts. It was concerned with subtleties of feeling and perception. Debussy, for example, avoided traditional harmonic and melodic patterns and incorporated an almost improvisational aspect to his music.

Impromtu

Impromptu, a short musical composition, usually for the piano, is another, smaller form of a classical style that can benefit the skeletal system. It has within it the feeling of improvisation. Many of the classical composers were famous for their impromptus and their improvisations. Beethoven, Mozart, and Chopin are just a few.

Selected Music to Aid the Skeletal System

Any music by traditional jazz artists would benefit the skeletal system, including the works of Miles Davis, Dave Brubeck, Maynard Ferguson, Louis Armstrong, Thelonius Monk, Charlie Parker, and the many early jazz artists.

The music pieces identified in the following table can also benefit for the skeletal system.

Music for the Skeletal System

Composer	Work	Effect
Gershwin	Piano Concerto in F	strengthens skeletal system; stimulates forward movement
Stravinsky	Ebony Concerto	rebuilds foundations of both body and mind
Grieg	Piano Concerto in A	stimulates new sense of balance; good for joints and forward physical and spiritual movement

MUSIC FOR THE SKELETAL SYSTEM (CONT.)

Composer	Work	Effect
Ellington	Night Creature	recovery, physical therapy
	Deep South Suite	strengthens bones and joints; flexibility
	Harlem	rebuilds body's foundation; benefits hips, legs, ankles
Brahms	Capriccio B Minor	strengthens balance, forward movement in life
Debussy	Ragtime for Eleven Instruments	strengthens body's major bones, skeletal tonic

2. TONAL AND INSTRUMENTAL THERAPIES

In Eastern traditions, the crown chakra is that level of the subconscious mind that most strongly influences the activities of the skeletal system. The crown center not only is linked to the skeletal system, but also influences the nervous system as well.

In addition, this center also works to balance the functions and activities of the brain hemispheres. Hemispheric synchronization has become more understood in the past decade or two than at any other time. In essence, when the hemispheres are balanced and working together, we learn more quickly and retain what we learn longer.

Music in the Key of B or B Flat or a Seventh

Specific tones and instruments are more likely to effect this level of the subconscious mind. Music in the key of B or B flat (major or minor) is very beneficial. If you are using a more personal scale, refer to the tone in the scale given for the crown chakra. Refer to Appendix B for additional information on how to create that more personal scale.

In the generic scale of middle C, the note of B or B flat is a seventh interval. Composers and musicians use the seventh in music to awaken feelings and to stimulate a sense of distance, giving the music a feeling of a new direction. The major seventh stimulates balance within the skeletal system. The minor seventh creates a kind of friction, generating feelings of new and unexpected doors about to open. Music in the key of the minor seventh is beneficial for joints and flexibility.

Droning and Orchestra Instruments

Droning instruments such as organs, bagpipes, Tibetan bowls and bells, and even quartz crystal bowls can be beneficial for the skeletal system, particularly in healing broken bones. Any orchestra instruments can also be helpful. Combination of instruments, especially with strong percussion and rhythm sections will be good for the skeletal system.

Music to Stimulate the Crown Chakra

The table below shows musical selections which are beneficial to stimulating the level of the subconscious and its corresponding chakra, influencing the skeletal aspects of the body. Remember to visualize the music surrounding you and then flowing into you through the crown chakra. See and feel it filling you and balancing the skeletal system.

Music for the Crown Chakra

Type	Composer	Work
key of B, B flat, both major and minor	Bach	Mass in B Minor
		Brandenburg Concerto no. 6 in B Flat
most traditional jazz music [2]	Chopin	Fantasie-Impromptu
	Mozart	Symphony no. 33 in B Flat
	Ellington	Harlem

---

[2] Traditional jazz artists include: Miles Davis, Dave Brubeck, Maynard Ferguson, Louis Armstrong, Thelonius Monk, Charlie Parker, and the many early jazz artists.

3. VOCAL REMEDIES

We can use toning, chanting, and affirming to help strengthen and heal the body's skeletal system. If you are unfamiliar with these vocal remedies, they are described in detail in Chapter 2.

Toning

The table at the bottom of this page shows the vowel sound and mantram beneficial for the skeletal system.

We can enhance the effects of toning, chanting, or affirming by using the appropriate musical key for the skeletal system. Use a pitch pipe or an instrument to tone, chant, and affirm in the key of B or B flat.

Playing healing background music in the appropriate key can also enhance the effects. Two useful pieces are Brahms' *Capriccio in B Minor* and Bach's *Brandenburg Concerto no. 6 in B Flat.*

Chakra	Vowel Sound	Mantra
CROWN	long e (*ee*)	om (*ohm*)

Affirming

Affirmations are beneficial to help heal and restore balance to the skeletal system. Some effective affirmations for the skeletal system follow:

I am supported by life!

I am balanced in all I do!

I face life with strength and ease!

I face life with courage and strength!

I am free of hindrances and obstacles!

I am receptive to all of life!

I move forward with joy and promise!

I move forward with balance and joy!

I face life with courage and strength!

I am fully supported in life!

Creating your own can affirmations can be very beneficial. Examine the emotional and metaphysical issues at play within your life that may be contributing to the imbalance. Also keep in mind the role and function of the skeletal system. It is our body's support.

WORDS OF POWER

Eheieh
eh-huh-yeh

"I am that I am"

This is the name of the Divine that is
the greatest we can know while
we are physical beings. It is also the
source of the Divine within us,
the structure and foundation for the
Divine potential within.

Metatron
meh-tuh-tron

"Angel of the Tree of Life"

Ratziel
rahtz-eye-ehl

"Angel of Hidden and
Concealed Things"

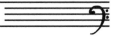
4. Music And Movement Therapies

A number of beneficial movements and postures can be performed with the music to amplify the healing effects to the skeletal system. As with all of the movements, they should be performed slowly and easily. Do not force, and don't be afraid to adapt them. Remember that all movements for the skeletal system should reflect balance and strength.

Their benefits are increased when performed against a backdrop of the appropriate music. For the skeletal system, choose one of the pieces of music listed or one that you have found personally beneficial. A nice slow jazz piece can be wonderful to perform with as can Chopin's *Fantasie Impromptu.*

In workshops, I teach an exercise for the skeletal system that involves series of movements. The first series of movements (A, B, and C) is performed twice. They are performed in the beginning and at the end. This series aids balance within the skeletal system.

Movement 1

Remember that as you perform this step, you are creating balance and steadiness within your body and your life.

Figure A

1. Stand straight and relaxed. Feet should be about shoulder's width apart, arms relaxed at your side.

2. With eyes looking forward, slowly raise one knee up so you are balanced on one leg (Figure A). Try and hold the balance for 15-30 seconds.

Placing a chair next to you to help balance is perfectly fine to do until you are able to balance without it.

Figure B

3. Slowly lower the leg, and repeat the process with the other leg (Figure B).

Movement 2: The Dancer's Pose

A slightly more difficult step, Figure C shows the traditional yoga asana known as the *dancer's pose*. If you are having trouble with balance, you may wish to skip this movement until you feel more comfortable.

Figure C

1. Begin with both feet on the ground. Then slowly raise one foot up, holding the ankle with your hand (Figure C).

2. Raise the other arm as you arch your back up, stretching forward and upward. Hold this position. Lower and repeat with the opposite leg.

   NOTE: If you are having difficulty, take is slowly, step-by-step. Only raise the leg and arm as high as is comfortable for you.

   As you become better at this, you may wish to take it even further, rising up on the ball of the foot as well.

Movement 3: The Tree Pose

Movement 3, known as the *tree pose* and it includes a bow exercise that I have adapted from Taoist traditions. This movement is the final step in the opening and closing series (Figure C). This posture strengthens and heals the bones.

Figure D

1. Stand with your feet flat and solid upon the ground.

2. Raise your hands above your head and lift your face to the sky (Figure D).

   See and feel yourself as strong and as balanced as a tree, with roots deep and strong within the earth and your branches extending toward the heavens.

3. Hold this position for 30 seconds and then lower your arms to your side.

4. Breathe deeply and slowly, feeling yourself more balanced and stronger.

5. Spread your feet wide apart and lower your hips a little.

6. Extending the right arm slowly out to the side, visualize yourself drawing a taut bowstring and shooting an arrow in that direction (Figure E).

    Exhale as you extend the arm, and inhale as you bring it back to switch arms.

Figure E

7. Repeat as often as you wish, at least 6 times for each side.

8. Repeat Movements 1 and 2.

This exercise can be the foundation for a lot of powerful variations. As we pull the bowstring, we can also tone or affirm, letting the affirmation fly like an arrow. Don't be afraid to adapt. Use visualization to help you as much as possible.

After performing Movement 3, repeat the first three balancing steps of Movement 1.

Notes

SUMMARY OF MUSICAL GUIDELINES FOR
THE SKELETON

Chakra	**Crown**
TONE	B (*ti*)
VOWEL	long e (*ee*)
MANTRAM	om
INSTRUMENT	Tibetan bells and bowls, bagpipes, piano, jazz instruments
STYLE	jazz, drones

Complimentary

Imbalance	Instrument	Key
aches	harps, sounds of nature	B, B flat
arthritis	orchestra	complete scale
bones	strings	B, B flat
teeth	strings	G, A

Skeletal Therapies

SOUNDS	COLORS	AROMAS
—	violet, indigo	lavender, clove, camphor
—	violet, indigo	lavender, lilac, sage
(*ee*)	violet, lavender, amethyst	lemon, lilac, lavender
(*eh, ee*)	blues, turquoise	clove

*Surrounded by the right sounds, we can
all be invigorated, energized and balanced.
It has been demonstrated clinically
that music adds to our general health and well-being.
Music, then, can be a important part of our
program of primary prevention—
the prevention of illness at the prephysical,
energy-imbalance level.*[1]

---

[1] John Diamond, M.D., *Your Body Doesn't Lie* (New York: Warner Books, 1980), p. 98.

Afterword

Sacred Sounds

Part of what the life experience teaches is that we have a responsibility to all aspects of ourselves. Certain natural laws govern all of life. We can only abuse and ignore the human body and our issues in life for so long before healing will not correct it—or it will become extremely difficult to do so. To enjoy good health, we all need a proper diet, exercise, rest, fresh air, and time to play. If we do not get these, the body will respond.

Sound is basic to all life, and although healing through sound and music will elicit some unique and individual responses, it will also affect everyone to some degree in a similar and discernible fashion. Regardless of the individual, sound and music therapy almost always induces a comfortable state of relaxation.

During the years in which I was performing sound and music therapy with individual clients, on only a handful of occasions did the individual not fall asleep during the process. Sound and music therapy are soothing and relaxing to body, mind, and spirit.

Ted Andrews   267

This releasing and relieving stress is the first—and one of the most important—steps in healing.

The second is remembering that we each can participate in that process. When it comes to sound healing, we can participate with great enjoyment. It only takes a little effort to experience its power—a little effort and a little trust. Sometimes it is difficult to trust what sounds good to us, but with music and sound therapy, when something sounds good to us, it is an audible clue that it is beneficial.

Our body knows how to respond, but we must help it. One of the best things we can do for ourselves is to get a piece of music for each system of our body. Public libraries are wonderful for this. Record 10 to 15 minutes worth of music for each system. These pieces then become our musical first aid kit.

We can then take time at the end of the day and look over the day's events. What emotions have we expressed or been exposed to throughout the day? What systems of the body do those emotions impact? By asking ourselves these questions, we can determine which systems and which organs have probably become stressed. We can take 20-30 minutes, and using our musical first aid kit, we can restore balance to those systems. In this way the stresses on those systems are not able to build up and eventually manifest as a dis-ease or health imbalance.

A number of composers have produced music that has the capability of balancing and healing all of the systems of the body. Most of these are the classical composers, but some pieces have been consciously written for those healing effects within our modern times, including my own composition, *Roses of Light*. The following compositions are just a small sampling of the classical music available that can heal and balance most systems of the body: Beethoven's *Ninth Symphony*, Liszt's *Christus*, and Holst's *The Planets*.

The sacred power of sound and music is still recognized and felt by everyone. Sound and music are contributing factors to our present society and our own state of consciousness. Music has an entertainment value, but it has a sacred one as well. It strengthens and uplifts us. Anyone who can respond to music can learn to use it to heal and to bless. Music can be a powerful physical and the spiritual tool.

All the masters that walked the Earth told their followers to become as children. It has been said that to be a child is to be open enough to hear the elves whisper in your ear and to know that the angels sing every day for each of us. But in order to hear the song of the angels, we must first hear the song within our own hearts. When we learn to balance ourselves with music and clothe ourselves in its healing sounds, then that song within our heart echoes throughout our life!

Appendix A

Frequently Asked Questions (FAQ) About Music Therapy

What is Music Therapy?

Music therapy is the application of sound, musical instruments, songs, compositions, and anything musical to assist in the well-being of an individual.

For What is Music Therapy Most Often Used?

Music therapy's most common use probably falls into the category of stress reduction. This is especially important since stress is a major contributor to most health problems and imbalances. Music therapy has been used in hospitals, educational institutions, nursing homes, and by private individuals.

Music therapy has been used for its anesthetic aspects, to relieve pain in hospitals and at home, to assist in the labor and delivery in pregnancies, for mood elevation and psychological balance, to promote physical rehabilitation, to aid relaxation and sleep, to facilitate learning, and in general to assist humans in almost every area of their lives.

Current research involves its application to physical rehabilitation, psychoneuro-immunology, and other areas.

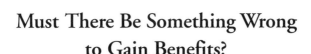

Must There Be Something Wrong to Gain Benefits?

Anyone, healthy or otherwise, can benefit from music therapy. People are exposed to a great deal of stress on a daily basis, and music therapies can relieve stress. Techniques may include combining music with guided imagery, simple passive listening, or even active participation in creating music.

What Kind of Research Exists?

In the past several decades, music therapy has become a degreed course at the university level. Much of this has to do with the continually growing volume of research regarding music and its applications within the medical and psychological fields. A little time spent in the public library will reveal a tremendous amount of rewarding information. Increasingly, over the past decade, research articles on music therapy appear within the *Journal of the American Medical Association* (JAMA).

Since the 1950s, several organizations have begun gathering, organizing, and reporting the vast amount of research available on music therapy. The following two organizations are the most notable:

NATIONAL ASSOCIATION FOR MUSIC THERAPY, INC.

(Publishes the *Journal of Music Therapy*)
8455 Colesville Rd., Suite 1000
Silver Spring, MD   20910

AMERICAN ASSOCIATION FOR MUSIC THERAPY

P.O. Box 80012
Valley Forge, PA   19484

Must You Have Knowledge or Ability with Music to Benefit?

Music therapy can be effective for anyone regardless of musical ability. An individual's experience with music does not affect the music's ability to have a healing impact. There are methods and tools and kinds of music that can be employed with anyone.

Is Classical Music More Healing than Other Kinds of Music?

There is no one single type of music that is any more healing than others. All musical types, rhythms, and instrumentations have their capabilities. In this book, I focus on a variety of musical types, including

classical, jazz, and folk music from other cultures. Any particular music I may have omitted does not mean it has no healing effects. It simply reflects that I either do not know much about that type or I did not have readily available information on it.

Frequently, I teach workshops on healing with sound and music. Invariably, someone will ask me about two types of music: country and rap. The assumption is that neither of these have healing abilities. Yet, country music has become extremely popular, and people are often found singing along with the music. Singing is a wonderful tool for healing, whether singing country, opera, or rock-n-roll. It opens expression and can aid communication.

Rap is one of the oldest forms of storytelling upon the planet. From the African griot to the Japanese zenza, rhythm and story telling went hand in hand. Stories were told universally with drumming and rhythms to heal and to entertain.

The kind of music that is most healing is often what we are most taken by, but it is important to remember that just as we need a balanced food diet, we will also be healthier from a balanced and variable musical diet as well.

Appendix B

Creating a Personal
Music Scale

The tonal correspondences assigned to the systems of the body throughout this book are generic. They are based upon the musical scale of middle C. This provides a construct by which we can begin to employ music to assist us in our own health maintenance. The problem that arises though is that we each operate on our own individual musical scale. While one individual may operate in the key of middle C, another may operate in the key of F. If we can determine our individual key, we will be able to impact more dynamically upon ourselves with music.

There are a variety of ways of determining our individual, musical key. One is through the astrological sign. Another is through our language, and yet another is through our vocal range. There are many ways of determining our individual keys and combining all of the elements to create the musical symphony that reflects our essence. For example, our name and our astrological chart can be converted to music, and since these are often considered by esotericists as our two strongest energy signatures, they are also the key to healing ourselves through vibrational methods such as sound.

For our purposes here, the focus will be on determining and using the musical scale associated with our own astrological sign. Many societies attributed specific tones and sounds to the various planets and the different astrological signs. Sometimes this was done through simply ranking the various planets and signs, and sometimes this was done through mathematics. Individuals such as Pythagoras, Ptolemy, Johannes Keppler and others developed their own correspondences. In music therapy, these tonal correspondences can help us to pin point a more personal and specific musical scale with which to work

The correspondences that follow are one of the simplest constructs, but they provide a starting point in working more individually with sound and music therapy. More specific information on determining and using our personal musical key in healing and higher consciousness will be explored in the forthcoming work, *The Songs of Enchantment*. By employing music in the scale of our individual astrological sign, we can impact more specifically to the condition that we may be experiencing.

Astrological Correspondances

Sign	Birth Period	Key
Aries	March 20–April 20	C
Taurus	April 20–May 21	C sharp
Gemini	May 22–June 21	D
Cancer	June 22–July 22	E flat
Leo	July 22–August 23	E
Virgo	August 23–Spetember 22	F
Libra	September 23–October 23	F sharp
Scorpio	October 23–November 22	G
Sagittarius	November 22–December 21	A flat
Capricorn	December 21–January 20	A
Aquarius	January 20–February 19	B flat
Pisces	February 19–March 20	B

Just playing music in the key appropriate to your sign of the zodiac will help you to align with your basic energies. Those into astrology can find some wonderful ways of experimenting with these tones and the tones of other important signs in the chart, *i.e.*, signs in which a great number of planets appear, the moon sign, the rising sign, midheaven, etc.)

CHAKRA

Base	Spleen	Solar Plexus	Heart	Throat	Brow	Crown
C	D	E	F	G	A	B
C#	D#	D#	F#	G#	A#	B#
D	E	F#	G	A	B	C#
E flat	F	G	A flat	B flat	C	D
E	F#	G#	A	B	C#	D#
F	G	A	B flat	C	D	E
F#	G#	A#	B	C#	D#	E#
G	A	B	C	D	#	F#
A flat	B flat	C	D flat	E flat	F	G
A	B	C#	D	E	F#	G#
B flat	C	D	E flat	F	G	A
B	C#	D#	E	F#	G#	A#

Appendix C

Imbalance Quick Reference

If you have a particular problem,
imbalance, or inherited tendency,
the table on the following pages
summarizes therapies and
references specific chapters
in the book.

IMBALANCE	SYSTEM	KEY	SOUNDS
abdominal cramps	digestion	E	*aw, ah*
aches (general)	muscular	D	*oh*
aches	skeletal	B, B flat	—
adrenal	glands	D	*oh*
allergies	glands	F, A	*ay, ee*
allergies	respiration	A, B flat	*ee*
Alzheimers	nervous	E, B	*aw, ee*
anemia	circulation	C	*oo*

INSTRUMENT	COLORS	AROMAS
flutes, woodwinds	yellow	mints
percussion, brass	pastel orange	lavender
harps; sounds of nature	violet, indigo	lavender, clove, camphor
percussions, rattles	orange and blue combinations	patchouli
harps, violins	indigo and orange	gardenia, eucalyptus
violins, bagpipes	indigo, red and blue	eucalyptus and gardenia combinations
strings, violins	violet and blue combinations; opposites, red and blue, yellow and indigo	rosemary, sage, thyme, violet
percussion	red	cinnamon

IMBALANCE	SYSTEM	KEY	SOUNDS
arthritis	skeletal	complete scale	—
asthma	respiration	F, G	*ay, eh*
belching	digestion	E	*oh, ah*
bladder	elimination	E, E flat, B	—
bones	skeletal	B, B flat	*ee*
bowels	elimination	D minor	*oh*
breasts	glands	F	—
breasts	reproduction	F	*ay*
bronchitis	respiration	F sharp	*ay*
circulation	circulation	C, F	*oo, ay*

INSTRUMENT	COLORS	AROMAS
orchestra	violet, indigo	lavender, lilac, sage
flutes	turquoise	eucalyptus, bay
flutes	yellow, citrine	peppermint, lemon
strings	indigo and orange combinations	lilac
strings	violetk, lavender, amethyst	lemon, lilac, lavender
blues instruments	orange, orange-yeallow	juniper berry
harp, cello, violins	pink, rose	rose, patchouli, frangipani
harps, cello	pink, violet	rose, lilac, patchouli
flute, violin	blue-greens	bay and eucalyptus combinations
percussion, bass	red and green	cinnamon, rose

Imbalance	System	Key	Sounds
colds (chest)	respiration	F, G	*ay, eh*
colds (head)	respiration	C	*oo*
congestion (lung)	respiration	F sharp, G	*ay*
congestion (nasal)	respiration	C, A	*oo, ee*
constipation	elimination	E	*aw*
cramps	muscular	E flat	—
cramps (menstrual)	reproduction	D, D sharp	*oh*

INSTRUMENT	COLORS	AROMAS
flutes, strings	turquoise, sky blue	eucalyptus, jasmine*
percussion (soft), orchestra	red, red-orange	eucalyptus
bands, orchestra	turquoise	eucalyptus
harp	red-orange	cinnamon, eucalyptus, bay
flute and strings, spiritual rhythms	yellow	rosemary, peppermint, lemon
shakahachi and Native American flutes	yellow orange	lavender
soft percussion, woodwinds	peach	pennyroyal, hyacinth, chamomile**

* Jasmine frequently stimulates the mucous membranes and may result in coughing up mucous throughout the night, along with stimulating sinus drainage which could interfere with sleep. Caution is advised.

** Caution should be taken when using chamomile as it is a member of the ragweed family. Some people may be sensitive to or have an allergic reaction to it.

IMBALANCE	SYSTEM	KEY	SOUNDS
diabetes (pancreas)	digestion	D, B	*oh, ee*
diarrhea	elimination	E flat	*aw*
ear problems	nervous	G, Gsharp	*eh, uh*
eye problems	nervous	A	*ee*
general conditions	nervous	complete scale	—
heart	circulation	F	*ay*
heartburn	digestion	E, F	*ah, ay*
high blood pressure	circulation	F	*ay*

INSTRUMENT	COLORS	AROMAS
strings, oboe, cello	violet	bay and eucalyptus
blues horns (trombone, etc.)	blue and orange combinations	nutmeg
reggae, harpschord	sky blue, blue and orange, turquoise	wisteria, eucalyptus
strings, violines	blue, indigo	eucalyptus, rosemary, pennyroyal, honeysuckle
strings (Baroque)	colors of rainbow	lilac, lavender, narcissus
strings, harp	green, pink	rose, jasmine*
orchestra	indigo	lemon, spearmint
strings, harps, violin	blue, green	rose, eucalyptus

* Jasmine frequently stimulates the mucous membranes and may result in coughing up mucous throughout the night, along with stimulating sinus drainage which could interfere with sleep. Caution is advised.

Imbalance	System	Key	Sounds
hyperactivity	glands	F sharp, G	*ay*
hypertension	nervous	A, B flat	*ee*
immunity	glands	A, F	*ay, ee*
indigestion	digestion	D, E	*oh, ah*
kidneys	elimination	D, E	*oh, aw*
liver problems	digestion	D	*oh*
low blood pressure	circulation	C, D	*oo, ay*
lymph	glands	A	*ee*
menstrual (general problems)	reproduction	C, F	*oo, ay*
nausea	digestion	E, G	*ah, eh*

INSTRUMENT	COLORS	AROMAS
harps, acoutic guitar	teal, blues, emerald	wisteria, eucalyptus
strings	indigo, violet	eucalyptus, myrrh
strings, violins	emerald, blues	rose, lilac, frankincense, sage
flutes (waltz)	pale yellow	peppermint
brass	yellow, orange	lemon
strings	lemon yellow	pine, juniper berry
percussion	red orange	cinnamon, sage
strings, cello	indigo, violet	lavender, sage
soft percussion	soft reds, blue-green	pennyroyal, hyacinth, patchouli
Native American flutes	ice blue	peppermint, nutmeg, wisteria

IMBALANCE	SYSTEM	KEY	SOUNDS
sexual energy (too much, too little)	reproduction	C, C sharp	*oo*
sinus	respiration	A, A sharp	*ee*
skin	nervous	complete scale	—
stomach discomfort (general)	digestion	E, E flat	*aw*
strain	muscular	D, E Flat	*oh*
swelling	muscular	G	*eh, oh*
teeth	skeletal	G, A	*eh, ee*
thyroid	glands	G, G sharp	*eh, uh*
ulcers	digestion	D, E	*oh, ah*

INSTRUMENT	COLORS	AROMAS
percussion, brass	red, fire tones	cinnamon, patchouli
strings,	red and blue	bay and eucalyptus combined
orchestra	pink	lilac, wisteria
waltz rhythms, chamber music	pale yellow	mints
woodwinds, soft percussions	peach	lavender, eucalyptus
strings, acoustic guitar	pale blues	lavender, wisteria, camphor
strings	blues, turquoise	clove
harpsichord, strings	sky blue, teals	wisteria, lavender
flute, woodwinds	blue and yellow combinations	nutmeg, peppermint

Ted Andrews

Appendix D

Composer Quick Reference
(includes music styles)

The table on the following pages
lists composers and their compositions which
benefit particular systems and chakras.

COMPOSER	COMPOSITION	SYSTEM/CHAKRA
Louis Armstrong	all music with Bessie Smith,	elimination,
	Basin Street Blues	BROW, CROWN
	trumpet music	SPLEEN
Johann Sebastian Bach	Brandenburg Concertos nos. 1 and 2 in F Major	circulation, HEART, CROWN
	Brandenburg Concerto no. 6 in B Flat	CROWN
	Fugue and Toccata in D Minor	circulation, SPLEEN
	Mass in B Minor	CROWN
	Contatas	circulation
	Jesu, Joy of Man's Desiring	reproduction
	Suite in B Minor for the Flute and Strings	SOLAR PLEXUS
bagpipe music	music in key of A and A flat, both major and minor	BROW

COMPOSER	COMPOSITION	SYSTEM/CHAKRA
Ludwig van Beethoven	Sixth Symphony in F Major (Pastorale)	circulation, digestion, HEART
	Fifth Symphony (Emperor)	BASE
	Moonlight Sonata (Sonata no. 14), Opus 27, no. 2	reproduction, SOLAR PLEXUS, THROAT
	Third Symphony (Eroica)	glandular (adrenals)
	Seventh Symphony	glandular (pituitary)
	La Sylphide	HEART, SPLEEN
	Ninth Symphony	nervous
	Creatures of Prometheus	SPLEEN
	Minuet in G	respiratory, THROAT
Hector Berlioz	Symphonie Fantastique	BROW
	blues music	BROW, SPLEEN

COMPOSER	COMPOSITION	SYSTEM/CHAKRA
Johannes Brahms	Symphony no. 1 in C Minor	BASE
	Liebslieder Waltzes	digestion, respiratory
	Symphony no. 4 in E Minor	SOLAR PLEXUS
	Lullaby	respiratory, BROW
	Capriccio B Minor	skeletal
celebrational music		BASE
chamber music	all music	SOLAR PLEXUS
Ray Charles	all music	elimination
Frederic Chopin	Nocturnes	glandular, THROAT
	Etudes	glandular, nervous, HEART
	Prelude in A Major	CROWN, THROAT
	Fantasie Improvisations	CROWN

COMPOSER	COMPOSITION	SYSTEM/CHAKRA
Aaron Copland	Four Piano Blues, Piano Fancy	elimination
	Quiet City	SPLEEN
John Coltrane	saxophone music	SPLEEN
dance music		SPLEEN
Miles Davis		SPLEEN
Clyde Debussy	Claire de Lune	circulation
	Afternoon of a Faun, Syrinx	skeletal, SOLAR PLEXUS
	Ragtime for Eleven Instruments	skeletal
drum music	primitive or modern	SPLEEN
Edward Elgar	Pomp and Circumstance	muscular
Duke Ellington	Mood Indigo	respiratory
	Night Creature	nervous, skeletal

COMPOSER	COMPOSITION	SYSTEM/CHAKRA
Ellington (cont.)	Deep South Suite	skeletal
	Harlem	skeletal, CROWN
Maynard Ferguson	any music	SPLEEN
folk instruments	droning	BROW
Franck	Nocturne, Symphone in D Minor	BROW
George Gershwin	Piano Concerto in F	skeletal, BROW
	Rhapsody in Blue	muscular, nervous, CROWN
Dizzie Gilespie	trumpet music	SPLEEN
Christoph Gluck	Dance of the Blessed Spirits	reproduction, HEART, SPLEEN

COMPOSER	COMPOSITION	SYSTEM/CHAKRA
Benny Goodman		nervous
Gounod	Valpurga's Night	HEART
Edvard Grieg	Piano Concerto in A	skeletal
George Frideric Handel	Water Music	circulation, glandular, respiratory, reproduction, CROWN
	Harp Concerto	circulatioin, glandular
	Messiah	CROWN
Coleman Hawkins	saxophone music	SPLEEN
Billie Holiday	all music	elimination, SPLEEN
Joseph Haydn	Symphony no. 85 (The Queen's Symphony)	nervous
Gustav Holst	The Planets	CROWN

COMPOSER	COMPOSITION	SYSTEM/CHAKRA
Mahalia Jackson	all music	elimination,
Scott Joplin	Maple Leaf Rag	respiratory
B.B. King	all music	SPLEEN
Ladysmith Black Mambazo	most compositions	HEART
Franz Liszt	Hungarian Rhapsodies	muscular, SPLEEN
Gustav Mahler	Symphony no. 1 in D Major	muscular, SPLEEN
	Symphony no. 4 in G Major	respiratory
Bob Marley	all music	CROWN
Felix Mendelssohn	Scottish Symphony	glandular (thyroid)
	String Quarter in A	BROW
	Violin Concertos	reprodution

COMPOSER	COMPOSITION	SYSTEM/CHAKRA
Milhaud	Le Creation du Monde	elimination
	Minuets	THROAT
Wolfgang Amadeus Mozart	Symphony no. 9 in E Flat Major	elimination
	The Magic Flute	SOLAR PLEXUS
	Symphony no. 29 in A Major	BROW
	Symphony no. 33 in B Flat	CROWN
	Symphony no. 40 in G Minor	respiratory
Carlos Nakai	all works	SOLAR PLEXUS
Pachelbel	Canon in D	SPLEEN
Charlie Parker	saxophone	SPLEEN
pastorales		SOLAR PLEXUS
primitive music		BROW
rhapsodies		SPLEEN

Ted Andrews

COMPOSER	COMPOSITION	SYSTEM/CHAKRA
Maurice Ravel	Sonata for Violin and Piano	elimination, SPLEEN
Camille Saint-Saëns	Bacchanalia from Samson and Delilah	reproduction
	Symphony no. 3 in C Major	BASE
Franz Schubert	Unfinished Symphony	nervous, THROAT
	C Major Symphony	circulation
Pete Seeger	all music	elimination
Richard Searles and Gilbert Yslas	Dance of the Renaissance, Dream of the Troubadours	circulation
Bessie Smith	music with Louis Armstrong	elimination
John Phillip Sousa	any marches	muscular
spirituals	all music	elimination

COMPOSER	COMPOSITION	SYSTEM/CHAKRA
Igor Stravinsky	The Rite of Spring	SPLEEN
	The Firebird	reproductive, SPLEEN
	Ebony Concerto	skeletal, nervous
	Piano Rag Music	respiratory
	Rite of Spring	SPLEEN
Johann Strauss	Tales from the Vienna Woods	elimination, digestion
	On the Beautiful Blue Danube and other Strauss waltzes	elimination, digestion
Peter Ilyich Tchaikovsky	The Sleeping Beauty	reproductive
	The Nutcracker	HEART
	Capriccio Italien	glands (reproduction, immunity)
Guiseppe Verdi	Triumphal March	circulation
Antonio Vivaldi	The Four Seasons	circulation
	Mandolin Concerto in C	BASE

COMPOSER	COMPOSITION	SYSTEM/CHAKRA
Richard Wagner	Ride of the Valkyries	respiratory, BASE
	Evening Star from Tannhouser	BROW
	Ride of the Valkyries	muscular
	Parsifal	nervous
	Tristan and Isolde	reproductive
waltzes		SOLAR PLEXUS
Wood	Harp of Brandiswhiere	HEART
Gilbert Yslas and Richard Searles	Dance of the Renaissance, Dream of the Troubadours	circulation
Zolden	Peacock Variations, Variations on Hungarian Folk Songs	muscular

Appendix E

Health Problems
by System

SYSTEM

PROBLEM / KEY x = affects X = strongly affects	Chapter 3 CIRCULATORY	4 DIGESTIVE	5 ELIMINATION	6 GLANDULAR	7 MUSCULAR	8 NERVOUS	9 REPRODUCTIVE	10 RESPIRATORY	11 SKELETAL
anxiety	x		x	x		x			
anger	X	x	x	x	x	x	x	x	x
anger at mate	x	x					x		
arrogance		x			x				
blame		x			x				
bullying		x				x		x	
conceit					x		x		
conflicting thoughts on sexuality			x				x		
creativity issues				x		x	x		
depression	x	x	X	x	X	x	x	x	x
disapproval		x	x					x	
doubts				x		x			
emotions	X	x	x	x	x	x	x	x	x
failure to move forward	x								
fears (general)				x		x			
feal of failure				x				x	
fear of letting go	x		X						
fear of progress and growth	x				x				
fear of past	x			x					
fear of future					x	x			x
feeling deprived		x						x	

SYSTEM

PROBLEM (KEY: x = affects, X = strongly affects)	Chapter 3 CIRCULATORY	4 DIGESTIVE	5 ELIMINATION	6 GLANDULAR	7 MUSCULAR	8 NERVOUS	9 REPRODUCTIVE	10 RESPIRATORY	11 SKELETAL
feeling misunderstood				x		x			x
feeling smothered							x	x	
feeling vulnerable		x				x			x
feeling unloved	x	x				x			
feeling unprotected					x	x			x
feeling unworthy				x				x	
frustration		x	x						
grief issues	x	x					x		
guilt				x				x	
hopelessness			x	x					
hypocrisy				x					x
inflexibility					x				x
immaturity			x				x		
impatience				x		x		x	
indiscriminate behaviors				x		x		x	
irresponsibility						x			
irritability	x							x	
insecurity	x				x				x
isolation						x			
lack of control			x			x			
lack of emotional nourishment		X			x		X		
lack of honor	x			x					
lack of insight				x		x			

Ted Andrews

SYSTEM

KEY x = affects X = strongly affects PROBLEM	Chapter 3 CIRCULATORY	4 DIGESTIVE	5 ELIMINATION	6 GLANDULAR	7 MUSCULAR	8 NERVOUS	9 REPRODUCTIVE	10 RESPIRATORY	11 SKELETAL
lack of responsibility		x		x					
lack of support			x		x				x
lack of sympathy	x			x					
lack of tenderness							x		x
lack of vision				x					
lack of will	x							x	
melancholy		x						x	
miserliness	x								
mistrust	x					x			
needing approval			x			x			
needing constant change	x	x							
needing recognition	x							x	
non-acceptance			x				x		
not expressing emotions	x	x							
nursing old wounds	x	x					x		
one-sidedness				x				x	
overly critical		x			x				
overly rigid		x			x				x
planning, but not following through	x	x		x					
poor self-worth		x						x	
possessiveness	x						x		
procrastination			x	x					

SYSTEM

KEY x = affects X = strongly affects PROBLEM	Chapter 3 CIRCULATORY	4 DIGESTIVE	5 ELIMINATION	6 GLANDULAR	7 MUSCULAR	8 NERVOUS	9 REPRODUCTIVE	10 RESPIRATORY	11 SKELETAL
sadness	x				x				
self-doubt	x			x					
selfishness		x	x						
sense of uselessness	x		x	x					
shame						x	x		
smothering	x						x		
stubbornness						x	x		x	x
suppressing emotion		x						x	
surrendering attitudes		x		x				x	
too dogmatic		x						x	
too judgmental		x						x	
too meticulous		x							
trying to do too much too soon	x								
unsympathetic						x	x		x
worries					x	x	x		

Andrews, Ted. *Sacred Sounds.* St. Paul, MN: Llewellyn Publications, 1992.

———— *How to Heal with Colors.* St. Paul, MN: Llewellyn Publications, 1992.

———— *The Healer's Manual.* St. Paul, MN: Llewellyn Publications, 1993.

———— *Crystal Balls and Crystal Bowls.* St. Paul, MN: Llewellyn Publications, 1995.

———— "Roses of Light—Healing Harmonies" (audio-cassette). Dayton, OH: Life Magic Enterprises, Inc., 1992.

Becker, Robert and Gary Seldon. *The Body Electric.* New York: William Morrow, 1985.

Benjamin, Edward. *The Restful in Music.* Boston, MA: Crescendo Publishing Co., 1964.

Bonny, Helen and Louis M. Savary. *Music and Your Mind.* New York: Harper, 1973.

Brusseau, Peggy. *Body Love.* Rochester, VT: Thorsons Publishing Group, 1987.

Clynes, Manfred. *Mind, Music and Brain.* New York: Plenum Press, 1983.

Crandall, Joanne. *Self-Transformation Through Music.* Wheaton: Theosophical Publishing, 1986.

David, William. *The Harmonies of Sound, Color and Vibration.* Manna del Rey, CA: DeVorss and Co., 1973.

Diamond, Johm, MD. *Your Body Doesn't Lie.* New York: Warner Books, Inc., 1980.

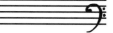

Feltman, John. "Healing with Light and Sound."
Prevention (June 1981), pp.89-91.

Gilder, Eric and June Port. *Dictionary of Composers and
Their Music.* New York: Ballantine, 1978.

Ginn, Victoria. *The Spirited Earth.* New York: Rizzoli
International Publications, 1990.

Godwin, Jocelyn. *Harmonies of Heaven and Earth.* New
York: Inner Traditions International, 1987.

Gutheil, Emil. *Music and Your Emotions.* New York:
Liveright, 1952.

Halpern, Steven. *Tuning the Human Instrument.* Spectrum
Research, 1978.

Hamel, Peter Michael. *Through Music to the Self.*
New York: Dorset, 1978.

Hart, Mickey. *Drumming at the Edge of Magic.*
San Francisco, CA: Harper, 1990.

Hawn, Jack. "Music Therapy: A Calming Influence on
Patients." *Los Angeles Times* (March 19, 1982),
pp. 18-19.

Heline, Corinne. *Beethoven's Nine Symphonies.* Santa
Barbara, CA: J.F. Rowny Press, 1965.

——— *Healing and Regeneration Through Music.*
Los Angeles, CA: New Age Press, 1978.

Ismael, Cristina. *The Healing Environment.* Millbrae, CA:
Celestial Arts, 1976.

Jeans, Sir James. *Science and Music.* New York: Dover
Publications, 1968.

Jonas, Gerald. *Dancing: The Pleasure, Power and Art of
Movement.* New York: Harry Abrams, Inc.,1992.

Gerontol, J. "Effects of a Music Theraphy Strategy on Depressed Older Adults," *JAMA*, vol. 273, no. 17, p. 1318.

Judith, Anodea. *Wheels of Life*. St. Paul, MN: Llewellyn Publications, 1988.

Lingerman, Hal A. *The Healing Energies of Music*. Wheaton, IL: Theosophical Publishing, 1983.

LLoyd, Norman. *Golden Encyclopedia of Music*. New York: Golden Press, 1968.

Loehr, Jim and Susan Festa Fiske. "Listen to the Music." *Tennis*, (March 1995), p. 34.

Mayo Clinic Health Letter. "Activity Therapy: Hobbies Do More than Just Pass Time," (August 1995).

McCarthy, Michael J. "A Management Rage: Beating the Drums for the Company," *The Wall Street Journal* (August 13, 1996), p. A1.

McClain, Ernest G. *The Pythagorean Plato*. York Beach, ME: Nicolas-Hayes, Inc., 1978.

McGarey, William, MD. "Music and Healing," *A.R.E. Journal*, vol. 11 (March 1976), p.92.

Marsalis, Wynton. *Marsalis on Music*. New York: W.W. Norton & Company,1995

Motoyama, Hiroshi. *Theories of the Chakras*. Wheaton, IL: Quest Books, 1981.

Owen, Robert. *You Don't Have to Die Sick*. Cannon Beach, OR: Health Hope Publishing House,1994.

Podolsky, Edward, M.D. *The Doctor Prescribes Music*. New York: Frederick A. Stokes, Co., 1939.

Retallack, Dorothy. *The Sound of Music and Plants.* Santa Monica, CA: Devorss & Co., 1973.

Scott, Cyril. *Music: Its Secret Influcnet Throughout the Ages.* New York: Samuel Weiser, 1969.

Steiner, Rudolph. *The Inner Nature of Music and the Experience of Tone.* New York: Anthroposiphical Society, 1983.

Schwarz, Jack. *Human Energy Systems.* New York: E.P. Dutton, 1980.

Tame, David. *The Secret Power of Music.* New York: Destiny Books, 1984.

Walter, Bruno. *Of Music and Music Making.* New York: W.W. Norton & Company, 1957.

Wilson, Annie and Lilla Bek. *What Colour Are You?* Northamptonshire: Turnstone Press, 1982.

A

acoustic guitar 153 195
adrenals 136 138
affirmation toning 48–50
affirmations for:
  circulation 74–76
  digestion 100–101
  elimination 124–125
  glands 148–149
  muscles 168
  nerves 189–190
  reproduction 213
  respiration 235
  skeleton 255
African rhythms 131 161 173
  204 219
air 223
allergies 14
altered state of consciousness 165
Alzheimer's disease 17 196
American Association for Music
  Therapy 274
anger 76
  See also Appendix E
ankle bone 243 244
anus 98 112
Apple Computer, Inc. 18
arm 244
arm muscles 158
aromatherapy 55–56
  See also Appendix C
arteries 57 61
asthma 14
asthmatic attacks 234
  beneficial music for 230
attitudes 48
  See also Appendix E

B

background music 50
bagpipes 145 146 263
Ballads 204
Ballets 205 219
Band music 231
Baroque music 40 64–65 83
  239
base chakra 44 70–71
  music to stimulate 75 210
  sounds to stimulate 73
bass 83 165 173 219
Big Band music 183 227
bladder 57 112
blood 60
blood vessels 61
blues 116–117 131 173 204
  219
bones 243 245 246
boogie-woogie music 71 83 161
bow exercise 260–261
bow pose 105
bowels 112 113
brain 57 177
brass instruments 129 131 219
breast 208
breath 49 228
breathing 223
breathwork
  See also affirmation toning
  See also color therapies
Bricklin, Mark 231
brow chakra 44 145
  music to stimulate 146
  sounds to stimulate 147
Burnham, Sophie 176

X

Y

Z

About the Editor and Book Designer

Pagyn Alexander-Harding and Diane Haugen provided the editing and book design for *Music Therapy for Non-Musicians*. Pagyn served as the project editor, indexing this volume, while finding appropriate clip art, and creating Appendices C, D, and E from the information contained in the original manuscript. Diane designed the book, assisted with the cover art, copyedited the final draft, and prepared the manuscript for camera-ready copy.

Pagyn and Diane are willing to assist others with their publishing efforts. Since both have self-published their own works, they can walk you through the publication process, help you to evaluate publishing options, including publishing on the World Wide Web (one of Diane's specialties).

Pagyn is a former technical writer who has taught journal writing and business correspondence to corporate professionals while working on a Master's Degree in Creative Writing. She specializes in coaching individuals on how to improve their written materials and is particularly adept in helping self-marketing authors or small publishers to develop marketing niches.

Diane's experience spans a number of different fields, from teaching freshman composition to working with authors in designing and editing books for publication. Her greatest strengths lie in her ability to use graphics as an organizing principle and her willingness to work at a craftsperson level of fine detail while tapping into the cutting edge of publishing technologies available today.

Pagyn and Diane may be reached at the following address:

IAAI, Hitterdal, MN 56552

(218) 962-3202

e-mail: hardings@ulen.polaristel.net.

World Wide Web URL for Whiskey Creek Document Design
http://www.rrv.net/wcdd/wc/welcome.html